EXECUTIVE
COMMUNICATION
POWER

FREDERICK WILLIAMS, a former president of the International Communication Association, currently teaches at the University of Southern California, where he was the first dean of its Annenberg School of Communications. In addition to consulting, he has lectured on communications for the United States International Communication Agency and has written several articles and books on the subject, including *Language and Speech* and *The Sounds of Children* (Prentice-Hall). He holds a Ph.D. in communications from the University of Southern California.

EXECUTIVE COMMUNICATION POWER

Basic Skills for Management Success

Frederick Williams

A SPECTRUM BOOK

PRENTICE-HALL, INC., Englewood Cliffs, New Jersey 07632

Library of Congress Cataloging in Publication Data

Williams, Frederick.
  Executive communication power.

  "A Spectrum Book"—T.p. verso.

  Includes index.
  1. Communication in management.   I. Title.
HF5718.W535   658.4'5   82-5435
ISBN 0-13-294157-0   AACR2
ISBN 0-13-294116-3 (pbk.)

This book is available at a special discount when ordered in large quantities. Contact Prentice-Hall, Inc., General Book Marketing, Special Sales Division, Englewood Cliffs, N.J. 07632.

10   9   8   7   6   5   4   3   2   1

Printed in the United States of America

Editorial/production supervision: Marlys Lehmann
Manufacturing buyer: Cathie Lenard
Cover/jacket design: Jeannette Jacobs

ISBN 0-13-294157-0

ISBN 0-13-294116-3 {PBK.}

Prentice-Hall International, Inc., *London*
Prentice-Hall of Australia Pty. Limited, *Sydney*
Prentice-Hall Canada Inc., *Toronto*
Prentice-Hall of India Private Limited, *New Delhi*
Prentice-Hall of Japan, Inc., *Tokyo*
Prentice-Hall of Southeast Asia Pte. Ltd., *Singapore*
Whitehall Books Limited, *Wellington, New Zealand*
Editora Prentice-Hall do Brasil Ltda, *Rio de Janeiro*

FOR VICTORIA

Contents

Copy This Form as a Handy Reminder
of the Basic Formula for
Motivation Power ("M.A.R.C.S.")

Permission to produce this form is given by the author and publisher. Frederick Williams, Executive Communication Power, *Englewood Cliffs, N.J.: Prentice-Hall, Inc., 1982.*

---

1. *Find the MOTIVES*

    - Find out about other people
    - Who are their "significant others"?
    - Use motives that healthy people respond to
    - Appeal to the highest motives

2. *ATTACK problems, not people*

    - Sidestep put downs
    - Don't waste energy on personal hostility
    - Make the other person feel good

3. *Get and give RESPECT*

    - Get your credentials out front
    - Show respect for the opinions of others
    - Be friendly

4. *Look for COMMON GROUND*

    - Find value bases for common ground
    - Consider shared personal experiences
    - Use the "yes-yes" strategy
    - Read and adapt to feedback
    - Try role reversal

5. *Use the persuasive SEQUENCE*

    - Use H3W as a planning aid

Preface

You don't need a five-hundred-dollar seminar to tell you that personal communication ability is a key to executive success. Look at those around you who are moving up in the managerial ranks. Too often we assume that outstanding communicators are born with that talent or are just plain lucky.

Wrong!

The fundamental premise of *Executive Communication Power* is that all of our communication skills, from giving a winning sales presentation to writing attention-getting letters, are learned behaviors. You can develop them, improve them, or lose them. Successful executive communication requires a positive self-concept (Chapter 1) and a knowledge of the strategies for motivating others (Chapters 2–6). It requires knowhow in meeting the challenges of everyday situations—from giving directions to handling office sex talk (Chapters 7–14). It requires regular tune-ups of the fundamental skills of speaking, listening, reading, writing, and even body language and memory (Chapters 15–20).

Your personal communication power can be visibly improved if you master these skills and conscientiously put them into practice. The few spare minutes a day needed to read *Executive Communication Power* should furnish you with the necessary understanding. You can do the practicing in time you already spend in everyday communication, but now you will be trying out your improved skills.

You can enjoy it all, plus move ahead faster on the road to professional success (Chapter 21).

That's what *Executive Communication Power* is all about.

1

TAKE CHARGE OF YOUR COMMUNICATION AND YOUR CAREER

As an executive, you may spend up to 80 percent of your time in communication activities, most of which can be identified with career goals. None of your communications, from memo writing to handling meetings, can be fully effective unless you know where you are going with them. This is the power of a positive self-concept.

1

The Power
of a Positive
Self-Concept

Effective modern communication is assertive. It is a powerful technique for influencing others in ways as mutually beneficial as possible to all involved. It is meant to create "you win, I win" situations. Communication power is the most valuable asset an executive can own. But you'll never know if you are winning with it unless you know where you want to go. Can you answer these simple questions: (1) Who am I and what do I want? (2) What does my organization want? (3) What do the people I work with want?

THE MAKING
OF SUCCESSFUL EXECUTIVES

Much has been written about how particularly successful individuals have gotten to the top. Some of what we read is cynical, such as the idea that the top is really the "top of the heap"—the bodies of those we have beaten out to get there. Some stories are mostly drama: the lucky breaks, or rags to riches. But there is consensus in most true-life stories as well as in the results of scientific studies that executive success is a combination of vision, the right skills, and a tremendous amount of hard work.

Vision is the ability to know yourself and your organization and where you both ought to go. It is based on your self-concept and an understanding of your organization, which are discussed in this chapter.

The right skills are your ability to share this vision with others, to motivate them to work with you rather than simply for or against you. This is motivation; it is the topic of Part II (Chapters 2–6).

Vision and motivation are not only fundamental bases of career planning; they are often underlying reasons for success or failure in every-day situations, from giving directions to idle chitchat. In fact, vision and motivation are gained and implemented only through communication.

SNAPSHOT VISIONS

The following examples are not unlike snapshots of the give-and-take that occupies our own lives. Certainly you could add a few of your own. But they are also examples of situations in which, if we explore in a bit more depth the personal attitudes and actions of the characters, we can see the manifestations of self-concept. We may catch a glimpse of the future of an executive.

It's the fourth time this month that Rita, the office receptionist, has been late getting to work. Elaine, her supervisor, is trying to decide whether:

1. *To read the riot act to Rita.*
2. *To skip over the problem because Rita has no sense of promptness, and to challenge her might be nasty.*
3. *To take Rita to coffee and explain why being on time is in her best interests.*

Elaine might, for example, read the riot act to Rita. Even if Rita were on time for a few straight weeks following such a confrontation, chances are that she would not only be nurturing hostility toward Elaine, but toward the company as well. This makes Rita the worst possible person to have as a receptionist. Moreover, every time Elaine tries to "solve" a management problem by staging a confrontation, she adds to her self-image as a negative, aggressive manager. Yet if she did nothing in the situation, her self-image would be one of powerlessness. She would be a living example of nonassertiveness.

Elaine's best alternative is to sit down with Rita and reason positively with her why it is particularly important for the company receptionist to be on duty on time. Elaine could try to find out if Rita has some pressing reason for being late and might offer some solutions. Just the act of trying to help Rita while being firm about her required schedule will result in the most positive benefits for everyone involved, including the company. In short, Elaine is trying to set Rita up for a "we all win" game.

Elaine would probably be called a good manager and a good communicator. She would be doing more than giving people directions. Elaine would be a positive and assertive communicator rather than a negatively aggressive or a complacent one. She approaches people-oriented problems with a "what can *we* do about it" strategy.

And if Rita were still late, Elaine would feel more justified in replacing her.

Amy, a hospital night-staff supervisor, wants a midyear raise. She knows that Franklin X., the chief administrator, already likes her work, so she wonders if she should concentrate her request on why a single parent needs more money.

Although being a single parent is a compelling and justifiable reason to Amy for getting a raise, it is a self-image that does not capitalize on the positive—that is, Amy's excellent reputation as the night manager. It confronts her boss with the possibly negative decision of favoring her over other employees who may have equally compelling reasons for needing more money. Moreover, this self-concept, especially if Amy is turned down, can sow the seeds of further negativism. Amy could feel that the hospital and Franklin X. do not care personally about her. Franklin might begin to believe that Amy is more preoccupied with her financial plight than with her work. They could become locked in an ongoing "no win" game.

However, Amy never got a chance to bring up her "single parent" argument. Her boss began their conversation by praising her work.

The point? Stress your positive concepts of self in negotiating with others.

Roger is a newly installed general manager in a small publishing house recently acquired by a large holding company. Part of his job is to change the senior editorial staff and give the house a fresh image. It bothers his conscience to be firing at least three people who have been with the publisher for ten years. What can he say to them?

The easiest but short-range strategy, and one too frequently taken by managers afraid to deal personally with people, is to say the least possible to the fired editors. Give them the proverbial pink slip. Do it on a Friday or before a holiday so you won't have to see them the next day. This is the strategy of managers who put themselves and their organizations far above and beyond the needs of the persons working for them. Although they may be good hatchet men (or hatchet women), their chances of gaining the type of employee allegiance that must underlie high productivity or creativity are virtually nil. Uncertainty sets up "no win" games.

Because people are important in his management style, Roger will meet with the three senior editors and explain what his directors have required of him. He will provide them the opportunity to resign, offer to help them relocate, and give them enough time to make their plans. This will take more time and resources than firing them outright, but Roger's image as a manager will benefit from it, and the remaining employees will stay more productive.

Roger's greatest personal dividend is that this overall people-oriented strategy helps him to avoid getting bogged down in difficult details of situations such as those described above.

For two years now, Bill has been a management trainee in the central office of a large cable TV company. Two other trainees—one who came a few months before him, the other about six months after—have been appointed to management positions in area franchises. Bill wonders if the company is trying to tell him something.

Bill is the victim of nagging doubts about himself. These are chipping away at his self-concept and could do so until his negative thoughts become a self-fulfilling prophecy. If Bill wants to gain a promotion and have the image of a manager on the way up, he is first going to have to believe it himself.

But even if he believes it, will they? He could sit back and hope that the company will see the light, then promote him. Or he could storm into his boss's office and demand a managerial appointment. The first alternative is another example of a nonassertive self-concept, as well as a one-way ticket out of management. The second might corner Bill's boss into a no-win game if there is no position he can offer him at the moment. In addition, a negative and aggressive style can lead to an immediate loss.

Bill does schedule a meeting with his boss. He decides to practice his plea for a managerial appointment with a close friend, who surprises him by saying, "Sure, what type of position do you want?" Bill is stymied for a moment as he gets his bearings. It was one thing to believe he was ready for management, but another to have some preferences.

The point? Clear up self-doubt by going positively to the source of your situation. Develop some priority scenarios. But be prepared to act on the answers you receive. If you have this overall strategy, then you won't spend time letting doubts chip away at your self-concept.

Bill does get the promotion.

Jeanne and Carol, both in their early twenties, are assistant managers of small suburban offices of a statewide bank. They are in the city tonight at a dinner honoring Ted K., about thirty-eight, who has been promoted to the position of vice-president for administration in central management. Carol is whispering to Jeanne.

"Isn't that Frank at the head table? What's he doing there? He's only an auditor in the downtown office."

"Didn't you know," whispered Jeanne, who knew both Frank and Ted personally, "they were roommates all through college. I guess Frank never got the breaks."

"Or maybe it's that Ted knew where he wanted to go," murmured Carol, thinking about her own career.

Moral: If you don't know where you want to go, how will you know when you get there?

TEN KEY QUESTIONS ABOUT YOUR EXECUTIVE SELF-CONCEPT

The following questions are not a test of any type, but a description of the qualities often associated with the self-concepts of managers, leaders, or executives. They are posed here as a basis for stimulating your thinking about yourself—both where you are now and where you want to go in life.

1. Do I know what I really want out of life?

Most leaders can reflect upon lifelong concerns with personal goals. They know that they want to be successful and they believe that they will be. Specific goals, such as being a doctor or corporate president, may change through the years, but there will always be goals.

2. Do my daily actions, decisions, or attitudes reflect what I believe are my major goals? Do other people know my goals from my actions? If not, why?

If your daily actions and thoughts reasonably reflect your goals, then you are in charge of your life. You are probably able to make decisions promptly because you have overall criteria readily in mind. If your actions differ from your goals, then one of two negative self-concepts exists: Either you are not in charge of your life and other people are running it or you are kidding yourself about your goals.

3. Do my goals include the desire to deal with others in mutually constructive ways? Do I generally try to set up "you win, I win" games?

This question is a gauge of your degree of people orientation in management. It is the feeling that people will cooperate with you if you treat them right.

4. In my communication, can I get others to understand in a mutually constructive way how I feel? Do I express well how I feel?

This question refers to the quality of assertiveness in your communication. It governs the degree to which your goals and strategies for acting in situations can be made clear, and often persuasive, to others. Lack of assertiveness is often the sign of a weak self-concept, a fear of failure in influencing others. Take care not to confuse positive assertiveness (where you are seeking mutual understanding) with aggression (where you are attempting to force others to believe or comply).

5. Do I stress positive qualities in my assertive communication?

The most effective assertive communication capitalizes upon what will be mutually positive to you and the other person. It sets up "you win, I win" games. Further, it avoids setting up a third party or the organization for a loss. Obviously, it is not always possible for everyone to have a total win. Positive assertion tries to maximize the best possible outcome. When conflict must be resolved, assertion then takes the form of negotiation.

6. Am I open to new experiences, willing to hear the other side out, or to change my mind if I desire to?

Open-mindedness is a positive characteristic of self-concept. It includes a willingness to change, to try the new, to be wrong, or to try the unpredictable. Individuals who are open to new experiences not only can adapt to organizational change, they can capitalize on it.

7. Do I have confidence in my decisions? Am I willing to ride out a situation for the longer-range rewards if I believe them to be worthy of the risk?

This question defines the contrast between the individual who always goes for the easiest rewards, even at the sacrifice of personal beliefs, and the person who holds out for what he or she believes to be right. It is not an unwillingness to change or to be blind to alternatives, but the exercise of a strong self-concept against the forces of undesirable compromise. This is *will power, persistence,* or *focus.*

8. Do I have the ability to perceive clearly what my organization needs from myself and others? Do I understand my role? Do I know ways by which my goals and my organization's goals can be mutually served?

The most successful relationship between individuals and organizations is when their mutual goals can be served by the individual's actions. The feeling of organizational understanding is vital to a positive self-concept as an executive.

9. Do I value my time highly? Do my actions show evidence of this value?

Time is among an executive's most precious assets. People who conscientiously value their time usually have a strong sense of self-worth. Yet we often see time squandered when low-priority items get high-priority attention, when schedules are not carefully planned, or when crises arise. If the dollars-per-minute costs (salary, overhead, lost time) of meetings were counted out with money on the table, chances are that these meetings would be fewer and briefer.

10. Does my self-concept have a game plan? Do I plan strategies for achieving my goals? Do I see myself as living a reasonably goal-oriented life?

Are your goals and your daily life connected in any strategic way? What could you be doing right now to improve your progress? Have you ever written out annual or six-month objectives, then returned to analyze what worked and what did not? (Chapter 21 gives you some ideas for goal setting.)

PEOPLE ARE YOUR MOST IMPORTANT BUSINESS

Once you know what you want and where you are going, your next most important challenge is to get people to work with you rather than only for or against you. You can achieve success in this by understanding and applying the principles of motivation, the topic of Part II of this book.

These principles will give you power with people.

They work!

II

THE BASIC FORMULA FOR MOTIVATION POWER

Getting other persons to want to do what you want them to do is the basic formula for motivation power. Most people will be moved to believe or do something if they sense the promise of personal reward or if they feel that persons important to them will want them to do it, or both. Your key to motivation power lies in your ability to stir up these motives in the other person. This is the heart of the persuasion process—and it works.

Here are five strategies you can use for the personal motivation of others. These are practical, easy to remember, and not difficult to apply.

- Find the *motives.*
- *Attack* problems, not people.
- Get and give *respect.*
- Look for *common ground.*
- Use the persuasive *sequence.*

Remember *motives, attack, respect, common ground,* and *sequence,* or *MARCS,* when you want your communications to hit on target!

2

Find the Motives

It's the other person's motives, not just your own, that are critical in persuasion. On a general level, people are moved by promises of personal reward and the approval of people important to them. All such motivation represents promised satisfaction of basic physical and psychological needs. Find the right motives and other people will persuade themselves.

MOTIVES THAT WORK

Your success in motivation depends upon whether the other person wants to do it. In general, what motives do we often see in everyday communication?

- The desire to behave in ways that are personally satisfying:
    "I like it."
    "I like getting a job done well."
    "Turns me on."
    "It's my job and I'm good at it."
    "I'm a pro."
    "I won't have to worry about that anymore."
    "That's a load off my back."
    "I'm moving up."
- The desire to do things that we feel people important to us would want us to do:
    "I'd never disappoint Mr. Johnson."
    "My friends expect me to be a professional."
    "Being on time counts around here."
    "My husband would love me for that."

Obviously, our most fundamental motives are ones related to physical survival—to stay alive, to be healthy, and to feel secure. But unless our physical survival is seriously threatened, we are not as persuaded by appeals to these motives as we are to more psychological ones. We often take physical survival too much for granted for it to be a good motive for everyday persuasion in our society. In fact, if we are threatened on the physical level, it makes for a special kind of negative motivation involving fear appeals. For example, employees usually don't spend a great deal of time thinking about their job benefits unless they are threatened with losing them.

Most motivation is positive and aimed at reward, growth, and achievement. This fits in well with modern humanistic theories of psychology, which hold that once our fundamental physical needs are met, most of our lives are much more occupied with fulfillment of higher psychological needs. We want to know who we are (self-concept), have a good feeling about ourselves, understand the world about us clearly and positively, and have the recognition of others.

Why all this psychology? Because it confirms all the more that the most powerful motives for persuasion are positive psychological ones. They are the substance of effective motivation—of getting the other person to want to believe or act.

You'll win if you find them and use them.

GET THEM TO SELL THEMSELVES

The new car bit . . .

A smartly dressed twenty-two-year-old tells the car salesman that he has just been promoted at the bank. He needs a new car. It must be little and cheap because he's budget-conscious. (The salesman acknowledges the small-car request, and also makes a mental note to offer dark color for banker image.) The young executive emphasizes that he's money-minded. (The salesman thinks about a small engine with high gas mileage, longer loan period for smaller payments.) The young man says he doesn't want to appear stodgy to his friends, especially lady ones. (The salesman wonders if the most expensive stereo tape deck will fit in this model.) The customer does most of the talking.

Eventually the right car is rolled out—conservative color, low payments, but plenty of image, including the stereo thumping out a deep rhythm. The new executive exclaims, "It's me!" Later he tells friends how hard he shopped to find the right car.

The young banker sold himself on the car, and any successful car salesperson will tell you that's how it works. The salesman was less concerned with the kind of car the young man initially asked for than he was with which motives would get the customer to sell himself. The basic sales strategy, as in the basic process of motivation, is to get the other person to want to make the decision. Both personal (self-reward) and social motives (admiration by others) are at work here. Note also how the motivating sequence operates. The salesman doesn't try to sell the car throughout the conversation. He lets the motives build up until the final moment.

It works.

Try These:

Find out About the Other Person

Take the time to assess other people. Find out their interests, circumstances, and possible reasons for acting or believing. Find out about their organizational status. What and who is important to them? Start your conversation by asking them about themselves. Ask others about them. If you are to meet with important persons from another organization, see if you can get résumés or bios. Do research on other people. Information is power.

Who Are Their "Significant Others"?

Find out who are the significant others to the person you wish to persuade. Will it be the boss, a wife, business associates, or close friends? Can you tie that "other" into motives for action? Remember, too, that you can be a "significant other" and one of the other person's best motives for complying with your wishes.

Use Motives That Healthy People
Respond to

Appeal especially to motives that are most important to psychologically healthy people. Abraham Maslow's (*Toward a Psychology of Being*)* list includes:

- having a clearer, more efficient perception of reality
- being open to experiences
- sensing the wholeness, integration or unity of oneself
- feeling alive, being spontaneous and expressive
- having a firm identity, a real sense of self
- having the ability to be objective, to detach oneself from the problems at hand, to transcend self and immediate problems
- being creative
- being able to shift between the concrete and the abstract; to see relations between the two
- to relate to the opinions of others, to be democratic
- having the ability to love

Appeal to the Highest Motives

In the 1960 presidential race, Richard Nixon promised to save us from communism; John F. Kennedy promised us inspiration ("Think not what your country can do for you but what you can do for your country").

Be careful with fear appeals. They stir up defense mechanisms ("Worrying

*From *Toward a Psychology of Being*, Second Edition, by Abraham H. Maslow. Copyright © 1968 by Van Nostrand Reinhold Company. Reprinted by permission of the publisher.

about cancer is for others"). People tend to avoid communications that might cause them discomfort ("Just tell me the good stuff this morning, it was a rough night"). Promises work better than threats.

Stop reading for a moment and think how you might use new motives tomorrow. It is when the other person puts the ball on the goal line that you score in communication power.

Remember that *motives* is the *M* in *MARCS*.

3

Attack Problems, Not People

Motivation works best when we separate people from problems. When we use negative motivation to put down others, we build hostility for which we may pay dearly later. Positive motivation not only has a better success record, but it lays the foundation for long-range personal and professional relationships. Attack problems; motivate people!

HOW TO WIN ARGUMENTS AND LOSE WARS

The Problem With Put-Downs

They backfire. You will seldom succeed in getting another person to want to do what you suggest if at the same time your actions are making him or her less of a person. When you demean another person, it is a direct attack on that person's concept of self. It is as if to say, "If you do what I want, it proves that you are as dumb as I told you."

You are setting yourself to lose in the long run.

Too idealistic, you say? Unreal? Consider the following case in point: Office wars . . .

Dolores was around thirty-five, divorced, with one child, and stuck pretty much in a senior secretary's job. She handled appointments and correspondence for the senior vice-president of an investment firm. A month earlier, the president of the company had hired Helen (around twenty-six, single, and a recent MBA graduate) as an administrative assistant. Among her duties was to supervise the secretarial staff, including Dolores. Heretofore, Dolores had answered only to the vice-president.

The new situation set up some obvious tensions, among which was Dolores's feeling that she had been demoted. It wasn't surprising, then, about a month later when Dolores blew up at Helen over a new dress code (no tight slacks, etc.) and a forthcoming Friday afternoon class on telephone manners.

Helen kept her cool in the meeting, saying that an increase in professionalism would have its rewards. But she did slip by saying that she sympathized—it probably wasn't easy for all the secretaries to dress better due to differences in income, family circumstances, and life-style. Dolores took this as a direct personal insult to her attempt to make ends meet as a single parent and to her lack of a college degree. This led to more clashes with Helen and finally to a private confrontation in which Helen told Dolores that if she were not professional enough to take orders, she could get out.

Dolores decided to take her medicine and live with the situation. It wouldn't have been easy at that time to change jobs, much less to move to change her child's school. She buckled down and did just what Helen told everybody to do. Helen even complimented her from time to time for "becoming" a professional. But there was still an inner resentment smoldering within Dolores. It kept her awake nights, and during the days she took every possible opportunity to put Helen in a bad light with her boss. She would remove a letter from the mail now and then, not forward phone calls, and even spread a rumor about Helen having an affair with a customer.

In a month they were both out of their jobs; Dolores was too ill to work for six months. Helen won the battle but lost the war.

Dolores's problem was not only her frustration with getting stuck in one job, but also in thinking that her status even there was now threatened. She blamed Helen, who for the most part wasn't accountable for Dolores's problems, save for her slip in sympathizing, which was taken as a put-down. Helen needed more of a "you win, I win" approach, and Dolores should have looked at Helen as more of a solution than a problem. She could have shared her frustrations and asked for help in working them out.

The point is that we have a natural human tendency to let our frustrations spill over from the basic source of our problems onto anything immediately associated with them. The back door sticks, so you kick the dog. Your office phone goes on the fritz, so you mutter about how the phone company rips us off. You get ticketed for speeding and gripe at the cop about all the crime in the city. This happens to everybody.

We need to unravel the *what* from the *who* in our problems.

These Will Help

Sidestep Put-Downs

When you see a put-down coming, avoid it. As they say in football, try for an end run instead of plunging through the line. Arguments mix people with their problems and usually set up "you win, I lose" games. Effective discussion, even assertive discussion (speaking out positively; see Chapter 1) keeps egos and problems more separate and can be used to shift confrontations to "you win, I win" games. Arguments that are postponed often cool considerably. Setting up a time and place to talk it out is usually to everybody's advantage. (Tip: Go out of your office to someplace pleasant—to a plush conference room or a terrific restaurant—and watch tempers cool down.) Winning an argument may give you some momentary feeling of victory, but usually all you have done is to unload your personal hostilities on another person, who may do his or her best to get back at you.

Don't Waste Energy
on Personal Hostility

If you sense your hostility building against another person, especially over a period of months, better try to defuse it before it explodes in a confrontation. If we are troubled over a sequence of events, it's not unusual to see them all associated with another person's doings. It's natural, but not usually accurate. We need explanations. We are attracted to explanations which take the blame off ourselves. Perhaps two thirds of all arguments are not due to the situation at hand, but to personal hostility that has built over a period of time. (Did he really walk out on his job because the boss questioned his travel expense account?) Don't waste your communication power in arguments when the real solution may involve venting some longtime frustrations which have little to do with the immediate confrontation. Try to analyze the underlying causes of arguments you might become swept up in. Find out how a third party sees it. Remember that you don't have to think you're crazy before you ask a counselor or clinical psychologist for advice.

Make the Other Person Feel Good

The better you can make the other person feel, the better the chances that you both will win. Try hard to see the other person's motives. "Kill 'em with kindness." Try to appeal to higher motives for getting along. Employ common ground as a motive (see Chapter 5). If the problem isn't that important to you, consider letting the other person win. Maybe it's more important to keep the friend and to lose the battle. It could win you the war.

Remember that the formula for personal communication power is getting other people to want to respond favorably to you. Doing them in is an empty win.

Attacking problems, not people, is the *A* in *MARCS*.

4

Get and Give Respect

Often we, ourselves, are a major reason for another person's actions, especially if we have their respect. The Greeks called it *ethos,* or persuasion due to character. Impressive credentials contribute to this type of persuasion. You can also get respect by giving it.

PERSUASION BY PERSON

You can be a major source of motivation when another person is wondering whether they should act on your suggestion. What was *ethos* to the Greeks is "source appeal" or "source credibility" in the modern world. Persuasion by credentials is the reason why most of us would rather believe our doctor than a faith healer about our back pains.

We can often be personally persuasive if we simply get people to like us. This is persuasion by personal appeal. You can attain it by showing an honest interest in other people.

Valerie was twenty-two, of seemingly fragile build, very attractive and feminine (not a sexist description but an important part of this story). She was within six months of graduating in mechanical engineering from a midwestern university. Her hope was to land a job in the design department of an engine manufacturing company just outside of Chicago, where she was now going for a final set of interviews.

The noon session would be the toughest. She was having lunch in a small dining room on the company premises with eight men from the design department. The company had never had a female employee in any job other than secretary. To be truthful, one reason they were interviewing Valerie was that the federal government had the company under the gun for not complying with equal-opportunity guidelines. Nonetheless, Valerie had the qualifications of an excellent engineer.

The luncheon had all of the makings of a disaster. She was late because her host from the personnel office forgot that the only ladies' room was two buildings away from the design building. The word had already gone out that the male engineers were going to have to take a female into their department. The men looked forward to the interview with feelings of mild hostility mixed with curiosity.

Valerie had dressed in a neat business suit, whereas the men were in their usual khaki pants and sport shirts. To top matters off, the rather embarrassed personnel officer introduced her as the "girl" they had been looking for, alluding to her petiteness (he thought it was a compliment), mentioned that she was single, and while introducing the men identified one as a bachelor. The looks on the men's faces ranged from blank stares to tight little smiles, as if to greet Valerie as the "girl next door."

Probably more out of nervousness than design, Valerie asked if the group could describe a few of their newest projects. She wanted to get them talking before the personnel officer asked the question that she had already heard too often: "Why did you decide to come into a man's field?"

The engineers started to talk shop and only stopped when one asked Valerie if they were boring her. She asked several technical questions and they got started again. After lunch she had the chance to meet with each engineer personally, gave each her résumé and a clipping of a technical article she had written for the student engineering magazine, and took care to keep the conversation going by asking questions about each man and his projects.

Valerie eventually got the job. The only company flap was over where to put the ladies' room!

She didn't give a damn.

Valerie's strategy was an example of persuasion by personal appeal. Rather than be defensive about being a female engineer, she concentrated on being a professional. She demonstrated active interest in the other engineers' projects and thereby earned their professional and personal respect. Valerie was her own best argument for acceptance into the company.

You've got to deserve respect in order to get it. But even if you deserve it, there's no guarantee others will get the message unless you help it along. How do you do this?

These Will Help

Get Your Credentials out Front

Don't hang your résumé on your nose, but don't keep it a secret either. If you are going to be introduced to a group, especially to give a presentation, never trust the memory of your introducer. Type out what's important on a small card and hand it over. You will be thanked, thought of as a professional, and the group will get the message. When you create an important document, consider including a final page on the qualifications of the author. If a friend is to introduce you to a new client or prospective associate, suggest what may be stressed in the introduction. In conversations, discussions, or presentations, don't be shy about giving personal examples that can boost your credibility. (But don't go overboard by using "I this" and "I that" too many times.)

Show Respect
for the Opinions of Others

Respect gets respect. It can set the tone of an exchange. Let other people get their points across. Try to understand them. Chances are they will return the courtesy. If you agree with even part of what they say, let them know. This develops common ground (see Chapter 5) or shared motives. Put your energy into telling your side of an argument rather than concentrating on just making the other person wrong. In fact, try to avoid telling other persons outright that they are wrong. Concentrate on the positive. Get the other person on your side.

Be Friendly

Address the other person by name and as informally as the situation allows. Body language (Chapter 16) is powerful, so smile. Avoid negative gestures. Keep your tone of voice as natural as possible (nervous men get loud; women get shrill). Be sure you are attacking the problem and not the person (see Chapter 3). Agree where you can. Try as much as possible to exhibit as genuine an interest as you can in the other person. Ask questions. Listen actively. Give friendly bodily feedback such as nods, smiles, and eye contact.

Try just a few of these suggestions and see if you can increase your personal persuasiveness. You might find yourself to be one of your own best arguments for influencing others.

Respect is the *R* in *MARCS*.

5

Look for Common Ground

Common ground in motivation power means pretty much what these words imply in everyday life. Do you and the other person have any similar motives for making a decision? Do you feel alike about something? Do you see anything the same way? Do you share any common values? If so, you can use these commonly held motives as a powerful persuasive device.

START WHERE YOU CAN AGREE

Birds of a Feather, Etc.

There is a fundamental principle in persuasion that the more two people, or a person and a group, perceive themselves to be alike, the easier it will be for them to persuade each other. Or just the converse is true. The more people perceive themselves as different from one another, the harder it will be for them to see eye to eye. This is sometimes called the missionaries' problem, because they are usually so different from the people they try to convert. It is also one of the basic problems in communication between people of different cultures, races, economic backgrounds, and even sexes. It seems to be human nature that if we do not have much in common, or do not know much about other people, we tend to be cautious in dealing with them. Sometimes we are subconsciously hostile.

But note that we said "perceived" difference. Given some exchange of information with another person whom we perceive to be quite different at first, we may see areas of agreement, of common concern. People may argue about the legality of abortion, but these same individuals will likely agree about the frequent tragedies of illegal ones. Members of different ethnic groups in this country may have opposite opinions about economic opportunity, but they probably agree that this country still offers the most individual opportunity in the world. Capitalist and socialist negotiators may be at one another's throats all day, but they enjoy the same classical music that night.

Grounds for agreement, even if removed from the issue at hand, can be a starting point for motivation. If you are able to get the other person to see that you share common motives, at least in part, your chances at persuasion increase accordingly. This is called finding common ground. It works all the way from direction giving (Chapter 7) to negotiation. Common ground is an effective sales strategy.

The Ways
Common Ground Works

Peddling persuasion . . .

Wally Samuels sells word processors. His best prospects right now are medium to small businesses, most of which do not have sophisticated office equipment. It's tough for Wally to get in to see the bosses in such businesses because they are usually covering two or three jobs at once. But it's only the boss who can make the "buy" decision. Moreover, most don't know or don't care about office automation. So if Wally does get in, what does he say?

> *Boss: Just leave your brochure. I'll call you if we ever get to thinking about getting into that sort of thing.*
> *Wally: Well . . . nobody knows your business better than you do. You're probably doing OK right now with regular typewriters. If I could just leave a couple of thoughts and my card with you . . .*
> *Boss: Uh huh.*
> *Wally: Excuse me, in the picture. Isn't that you with the touring bike?*
> *Boss: Why, yes . . . you must know long-distance biking.*
> *Wally: Yes, sir. I finally got up to a custom frame and all Campagnolo gear.*
> *Boss: That's "Campy" gear in the picture. Problem is I can't find a shop that carries it around here.*
> *Wally: Would you like a catalog from a real reliable supply house?*
> *Boss: Well . . . sure . . . that's real thoughtful of you.*
> *Wally: About the word processors. In addition to increasing typing productivity about fifty percent, think about these two additional benefits. First . . .*

Wally left his card and sent the Campagnolo catalog about a week later with another card attached and a snapshot of him on his touring bike. Eleven months later he even remembered to send a new edition of the bike-parts catalog, along with a flyer on a new word processing line.

When the boss was ready to think about getting into word processing,

Wally was the first person he called. Wally made the sale and got two referrals to boot!

Sound too simple to work? Well, it did. Wally got on common ground first by agreeing with the boss that he didn't need a word processor at the moment. He also staked out important common ground when he noted their shared interest in bicycle touring.

Common ground is also a powerful component of "you win, I win" persuasive strategies. Automatically, you both share a motive to win.

These Work

Find Value Bases
for Common Ground
Beyond the issue of the moment, consider the beliefs or values you may share with the other party. In any honest approach to a problem situation (i.e., where someone is not trying to do you in), you and the other person will have a shared desire to see the problem clearly. You will want to respect one another's opinions. You can both acknowledge that you will be better off if you get something positive accomplished. (This is a bid for a "you win, I win" game.) Often, in naturally antagonistic situations (seller and buyer, Republican and Democrat, competitive companies, plaintiff versus defendant), there is common concern to preserve the system under which you operate. Sellers need buyers. Democrats and Republicans need the two-party system. Business competition can heat up the market. The justice system is based on legal recourse for the resolution of disagreements.

Consider Shared Personal Experiences
as Common Ground
As in the example of Wally, look for experiences you may hold in common with others. These can be as general as having both been in the armed forces at a particular time, having children the same age, having visited a certain city or country, having the same kind of automobile, playing the same sport, following the same team, or having a common hobby. This type of common ground is less powerful than shared values, but it is a starting point.

Use the "Yes-Yes" Strategy
to Generate Common Ground
Create common ground on the spot by offering a series of statements which will prompt a series of yesses from the other person. One yes will tend to lead to another.

We humans have a fundamental tendency to want to experience agreement rather than disagreement. Most people would rather say yes than no. A "no" response sets up an automatic challenge; we may have to back it up. It is more emotionally expensive. "Yes" is easier for us to give or to get. "Yes-yes" sequences also have a cumulative effect. A "yes" on one point contributes to the expectation of a "yes" on the next. For example:

"Look, we are both in this together."

"Yes."

"And we'd both like to come out ahead."

"Yes."

"Otherwise we may end up paying our lawyers more than this whole thing is worth to either of us."

"Yes."

A "yes" isn't guaranteed at this point, but there is a greater probability of it because of the yesses leading up to the proposed resolution.

Read and Adapt to Feedback

As you attempt to persuade another person, watch carefully for feedback, especially from body language (see Chapter 16). Try to keep yesses coming, even if they are in the form of nods, "uh huhs," or friendly eye contact. Even the lack of an outright no may often mean a mild yes or a maybe. Adapt your remarks to keep positive feedback coming. Simply adapting to the other person and maintaining a positive interaction will contribute to common ground.

There is a law professor who compares the process of appealing to a jury to driving his car down a country road. He knows where he wants to go in his remarks and as long as he gets positive or neutral feedback from the jury, he stays on the same road. But the minute the "no" looks start coming, he slows down and tries turning one way or another until he knows that he is back on a positive track with the jury.

You can train yourself to read feedback better than you do now. Also, what kind of feedback do you give? If you are really serious about this, ask a friend or look at a videotape of yourself. Most people cannot believe that they give off so many feedback cues.

Try Role Reversal

Put yourself into the other person's shoes to see if you can sense how that person would feel in a situation. Then use this feeling as a basis for developing common ground. Role reversal is a serious strategy for determining how other people feel. Some clinical psychologists use it to iron out family or marriage differences. Consider setting up a mock situation where a colleague plays your role and you play out the responses of your opposing party. The insights will surprise you. They can be powerful bases for developing common ground.

Trying to see a problem from another point of view can free you a little from your own biases. It also gets you to make generalizations about the other person's attitudes. Just the act of role playing forces you to transcend the problem for the moment, sometimes making potential common ground evident. In some situations you can try role reversal directly with the other person involved. I know business partners who, with a consultant's help, used role reversal to untangle personal antagonisms that were breaking up their professional relationship.

Role reversal is an excellent exercise for developing your empathetic ability—that is, your ability to experience personally another person's feelings. Persons with a high empathetic ability tend to be excellent one-on-one communicators. This is an especially powerful talent for individuals working as consultants who must adapt daily to whole new sets of clients.

All of these common-ground tactics will work for you at one time or another. Practice them in low-risk situations with friends or family. You'll then be ready to use them powerfully when the results are especially important to you.

Common ground is the *C* in *MARCS*.

6

Use the
Persuasive Sequence

Motivation seldom operates as a one-shot, "you give it, they get it" process. It is more complex. The psychological components of the persuasive process include (1) getting attention, (2) making it clear what you want, (3) stirring up motives why the other persons should act, and (4) letting them know when you want the action. When put into action, these comprise the persuasive sequence.

THE "H3W" FORMULA

The persuasive sequence combines the psychological components which move people to belief or action. It's persuasion as it comes alive in our communications. These components go by many different names in various theories of persuasion, but for simplicity's sake, why don't you remember them as:

Hey!: getting attention
What?: stating what you want
Why?: appealing to the other person's motives
When?: specifying when you want the action

You can easily remember these critical components as the "H3W" formula. It's especially handy to be sure you have covered all the necessary points in a presentation, a letter, or even a brief announcement. How many times have you seen the following happen?

28

EMPLOYEE BENEFITS MEETING
Find out about stock sharing, health plans, and the new retirement accounts.
This is our most important meeting of the year!
See you there.
Room 6.

J.J.

OK, J.J.—but when?
Or how about this one?

Worker: The people up in B2 just dump their requisitions in our department in-basket like they couldn't care less about all the work we had to do.
Supervisor: People are getting so darned inconsiderate these days.
Worker: My desk was broken into last week.
Supervisor: Just like I said—inconsiderate!
Worker: Just look at that mess over there.
Supervisor: What was it you wanted, anyway?

It's not unusual to get so wrapped up in an immediate situation that we forget to include the vital What? in our directions. You can avoid such problems by remembering and applying the H3W formula.

To make motivation work, you usually must accomplish all of the Hey! What? Why? and When? of the persuasive sequence. If you are good at reading feedback, you can check on them as you are talking, then go back and redo any that haven't worked. Obviously, some may be more important than others at times, but most instances of effective communication combine them all.

Some Tips

Use H3W as a Planning Aid
Use the H3W formula as a guide for planning a presentation. The Hey! is your introduction, the What? Why? and When? comprise the main body of your remarks, then a quick review of H3W is an effective conclusion.

Use Feedback to Check on Your H3W
During the persuasive process, check on your success in holding attention, securing understanding and acceptance of your objectives, and see if your When? is clearly grasped. Like the earlier example (in Chapter 5) of the law professor who compared speeches to juries with driving down a country road, use feedback to make mid-trip corrections. Keep the formula in the back of your mind not only when you plan your presentations, but during them. H3W is a great road map.

Use Plenty of HEY'S!

Plan on different types of Hey's! for your presentations. Ask questions. Address people by name. Ask for reactions. Use attention-getting facts. Employ striking visual aids. In your correspondence, address people by name in the text of the letter. Use signposts such as "Here's the crucial issue, Harry . . ." Try graphics (underscoring, arrows, bold type). Remember that none of the components of the persuasive sequence will do anything for you if you are not holding the other person's attention.

Use H3W as a Check
on Communications Directed to You

When someone else is giving you an important message, check on its completeness. Are you clear on the What? Do the Why's make sense? When should you act? Then get the missing parts before it's too late.

Make Your WHEN's?
Especially Effective

The more concrete the When, the more effective it will be.

Although it is easier for people to make a momentary commitment to what you want if the When? is fuzzy, such commitments fade fast. State the When? precisely ("Call me at ten tomorrow morning").

> The sooner the other person can do the When?, the better are your chances of getting action.

If you are getting members of a group to volunteer for various duties, get them to sign up on the spot. Tell them that they can change later, but get the commitment on the dotted line immediately. (Ever see how easy it is to make a pledge at a fund raiser?)

> Keep the responsibility for the When? in the other person's hands. Get that person to feel that the next step is theirs, not yours. ("If you will send me a check by Monday, I'll buy the plane tickets for any of you in this group and you'll get a better rate.")

Try this experiment the next time you are getting a group to decide on a future meeting time. First, say: "Let's get in touch when we've had a chance to check our calendars." About ten seconds later, say: "I'll call you to see when our best meeting date would be." Then about ten seconds after that, say: "Better yet, check your calendar Monday and call me about which meeting date would be best for you." Notice that on this third request most people will make a note of what they are supposed to do. The When? ball is directly in their court. They are obligated to act.

> Try using When's? that people can act on immediately. Psychologists call this a "releaser stimulus."

A releaser stimulus is what happens when an evangelist gets a crowd in a frenzy, then says, "Stand up for God!" Or when, after a pep talk at a fund raiser, the organizers hand out pledge cards. (It's easier to give that way, isn't it?) TV commercials use the same tactic. ("Call now! 1-800-743-2222 and we'll have your vegetable chopper in the mail tomorrow! Act now!") A releaser stimulus lets you trigger the When in the other person. The What and the Why are built up to the point where people are ready to act. Then you make it as easy as possible for them to respond right on the spot.

The persuasive sequence makes motivation work. Every day of your life people are using it on you. You'll profit by knowing how it works and even more by putting it to work for yourself. Remember—H3W.
Sequence is the *S* in *MARCS.*

COPY THIS PAGE
AS A HANDY REMINDER OF THE BASIC FORMULA
FOR MOTIVATION POWER (MARCS)

1. Find the *motives*
   - Find out about other people
   - Who are their "significant others"?
   - Use motives that healthy people respond to
   - Appeal to the highest motives

2. *Attack* problems, not people
   - Sidestep put-downs
   - Don't waste energy on personal hostility
   - Make the other person feel good

3. Get and give *respect*
   - Get your credentials out front
   - Show respect for the opinions of others
   - Be friendly

4. Look for *common ground*
   - Find value bases for common ground
   - Consider shared personal experiences
   - Use the "yes-yes" strategy
   - Read and adapt to feedback
   - Try role reversal

5. Use the persuasive *sequence*
   - Use H3W as a planning aid
   - Use feedback to check on your H3W
   - Use plenty of Hey's!
   - Use H3W on communications directed to you
   - Make your When's? especially effective

Permission to reproduce this page is given by the author and publisher. Frederick Williams, Executive Communication Power, *Englewood Cliffs, N.J.: Prentice-Hall, Inc., 1982*

WIN IN THE EIGHT MOST TYPICAL SITUATIONS

Most of our communications challenges in organizations fall into regular categories. We are often left to learn slowly from experience how to react to these challenges. Why not get a jump ahead by learning from the experiences of others? How long can you afford to communicate at less than your full potential?

7

Giving Directions

The deceptively simple task of giving directions is far more important than most managers think. The age of blind faith is over. You have to motivate as well as administrate. Employees will be ready to act for you or against you. Are you only a direction giver and not a manager? Do you tend to confuse people with things? Learn the five steps for giving successful directions. Troubleshoot your own style as a direction-giving executive.

PEOPLE VERSUS THINGS

Giving directions is more than just telling people what to do.

Harper Phillips was twenty-eight and just completing a miserable first year as the manager of a technology assessment group in a middle-size aerospace firm. The year was especially disturbing to Harper because for five years he had been a star young engineer in the firm. Raises had come along on schedule, and so had an unexpected midyear bonus from time to time. Unexpected also was the fact that when Harper was given an early break to move into management, his life became miserable. People seemed to resent his giving them directions. Although they acknowledged his orders, they appeared to do the least possible work to get by. Even his secretary regularly got on his nerves, so much so that he had her put on probation.

All this made Harper perpetually tired and irritable. His dissatisfaction with people carried over to his home life. His wife and kids seemed to avoid listening to him. One day Harper even reached the point of writing out a list of directions for his family and going over it as they sat down to dinner! This, of course, spoiled dinner for everybody. Eventually Harper went back into straight engineering work, where he began to feel happy again. Harper assumed that he was not cut out for management—nor for the higher executive ranks.

35

Harper's conclusion was unfortunate because his basic problem was a simple one: He had tried to manage people the same way he had successfully managed things. People need more than direction—they need motivation; they need to want to respond to directions. The difference between Harper's spending his career over a drafting board instead of in the executive suite was a matter of knowing how to apply a few fundamental principles of giving directions that motivate compliance.

Five Steps for Successful Directions

Step One: Be Clear in Your Own Mind What You Want Accomplished and Who Should Do It

Many directions fail because givers are not clear themselves on what they want and why they want a particular person to do it. They have not sufficiently thought through the objective and its consequences.

Ask yourself precisely what your objectives are and where they fit in your overall management scheme. Will this be a regular task to be delegated; will whoever does the job be expected to do it in the future as a regular routine? If so, be sure that you know what you want and the best way to get it, because you are also setting up policy. Or is it a one-time task? Then it may be especially important to explain to the person doing it why he or she has been selected.

Check your reasons for selecting the person you chose for the task. Are you training a new person for the job? If so, then assume that it may take more time and you may have more mistakes than if your most capable person were doing it. Be ready to communicate the training reasons when you give the directions. Consider, also, what the person will need in order to do the task—special paperwork, travel, materials, phone numbers, including time off from another activity.

Step Two: Select the Best Medium for Communicating Your Directions

Know the relative advantages and disadvantages of the different media for giving directions. Often combinations are most effective for important tasks.

Consider the following advantages and disadvantages of the typical media for direction giving.

Person-to-Person: Directions have a personal quality in face-to-face communication. You can obtain immediate feedback and go on, if necessary, to clarify. In-person communication is by far the most effective medium for motivation. Also, it is especially helpful if individuals can participate in formulating the directions with you. This builds personal commitment. However, without a follow-up memo, there is no record of your spoken directions; no reminder or directive to refer back to if directions are forgotten. (Tip: People on their way up will often carry a small notebook to important meetings for jotting down directions given by superiors. It's impressive and it works.)

But take care; personal communication can be time-consuming. Also, either you or the other person may be in the wrong mood to be maximally effective at that moment.

Telephone: Use of a telephone has a personal quality (although less than face-to-face communications), and saves time and the need to get together with the other person. As with person-to-person speech, you can obtain immediate feedback and clarification. But there is no record. You cannot observe how a person is reacting (body language, Chapter 16) to your directions. Also, we are often trapped into accepting telephone calls at times when other matters are distracting us.

Meetings: This is a particularly effective medium when directions involve the necessary cooperation of a group of individuals. It permits interaction over the directions and perhaps modifications for the better. Meetings are the main medium of participatory management; they build commitment to decisions. But meetings are time-consuming and expensive. Sometimes an individual or an event can get in the way of effective group communication (see Chapter 12).

Memos and Directives: These provide the often necessary record of the direction, not only for you and the other person, but also for the information of other interested individuals. It is more difficult to make a memo as motivational as face-to-face communication. Worse yet, memos do not give you immediate feedback unless followed up with a meeting or telephone call. They are very one-way.

Step Three: Motivate
as Well as Direct;
Get Acknowledgment

The more personally you motivate, as compared with basing your request only upon job requirements, the greater the probability that important directions will be followed. Remember *MARSCS* (Chapters 2–6): (1) Find the motives. (2) Attack problems, not people. (3) Get and give respect. (4) Look for common ground. (5) Use the persuasive sequence.

Are your directions clear and complete? Do they include the Hey! What? Why? and When? components of the persuasive sequence? (Remember H3W in Chapter 6.)

Never assume that directions are understood the first time around. Try as much as possible for immediate feedback. (If it's a memo situation, ask for confirmation by phone or, if you have the time, by a return memo.) Always get acknowledgment. If it's a critical task, get a second acknowledgment later.

Step Four: Evaluate Progress

If it's important, ask for interim progress reports. Don't overlook the possible need to revise the task or its methods of accomplishment. Have in mind what to do if progress is slowed or if completion is not going to be in line with your objectives.

Consider a schedule of informal contracts to review progress—telephone calls, notes, or informal visits.

Step Five: Evaluate
and Give Feedback
Upon Completion

How many times have you worked ceaselessly on a task, with much up-front motivation from a superior, only to have its completion greeted with silence (or a new task!)?

Obviously, if the task you assigned was difficult or important, remind yourself to bestow a visible reward. This can range from a letter or memo to a pay bonus or promotion. It's critical at least to acknowledge completion.

If the task involved learning a new procedure or skill, acknowledge how accomplishment fits into the individual's professional growth. Identify the next steps for growth. The psychological association of task completion and personal success is among the most powerful means for relating the goals of an organization to the goals of an individual. It is highly motivational.

Feedback can also incorporate evaluation. What worked well? What could be improved next time? Constructive criticism improves your methods for getting jobs done. It can also be taken by an individual as a contribution to professional growth. Don't overlook asking the person doing the task to do some of the evaluating.

Troubleshooting Tips

Use the following five questions as a basis to check on problems you may have in giving directions. There are no totally right answers, but the items will get you thinking.

1. Do you find yourself wondering why people working for you cannot listen better?

> See whether lack of listening may be due to your lack of including motivation in your directions. Also, follow up your conversations and meetings with memos.

2. Do you perpetually find that people cannot quite get the job done right and that you tend to expect failure?

> Check on whether your expectation of failure is subconsciously moving you to set people up for it as a confirmation of your expectations. This sounds implausible but it happens. Remedy: Go over directions with the other person. Work out agreements that they feel will be possible to accomplish. This builds commitment and lets you avoid trapping them in a no-win situation.

3. Are there some people, particularly of the opposite sex, of a different age group from you, or from certain minority groups, who just don't seem to be able to take your directions?

> Ask yourself whether you are making the wrong assumptions about motivating certain types of people. Perhaps you are using what they consider to be negative stereotypes. Find out what motives are important to different types of individuals who work for you. Better yet, motivate them as individuals, not as types.

Some men take a lot of static from their wives when they find themselves working for a woman boss. This makes "family" or "wife" a touchy subject for personal motivation. Women get tired of either being classed as feminine and not professional, or as professional and not feminine. The successful woman in business combines both traits. Members of ethnic groups often detest being compared only to success symbols restricted to their respective group. Too often age is looked upon as a handicap rather than an asset.

Look out for stereotypes in your motivation.

4. Do you find that if jobs are not done completely or correctly, you never hear about it until it's too late?

> Examine whether you are taking a sufficiently active role in requesting progress reports, even bad-news ones. People are smart enough to know that bad news does not bring rewards. Get your employees to know that you want to attack problems, not people. Give rewards for timely reports. Take a "we" approach with your employees toward solving problems and getting a job done.

5. Even when others seem highly motivated to get jobs done, are there still inaccuracies, oversights, and delays?

> Check the clarity and completeness of your directions. Often we give directions so frequently that we take it for granted that they are understood. Are you assuming too much knowledge on the part of the person picked to do the job? Use feedback to find out. Follow up face-to-face direction giving and meetings with memos. Ask for progress reports. Being interactive in giving directions and receiving reports will aid the situation.

8

Getting Up
in Front of People

If you are not at least a little anxious when standing up before an audience or even a small group, you've either done it too much or you're emotionally dead. It is normal to be nervous when you get up to speak, even if only to say your name, so expect it. The winning strategy is not to repress nervousness through use of tranquilizers or alcohol, but to channel it into energizing what you have to say. If you show some excitement, it will be contagious and will work in your favor. The jitters can be the least of your worries.

CAN YOU RISE
TO THE OCCASION?

Any one of us, if we are ever to communicate to more than one person at a time, must face speaking before a group. It might be to answer a brief question at a meeting. We may be called upon to give a major presentation—perhaps such an important one that it could make or break our career. Why is it, then, that if we do very little speaking, we are as apt to be as nervous at a small meeting as we are in front of a hundred people?

The answer is straightforward. All of us want to be seen favorably in the eyes of others. It's a basic human psychological need. This need is never so evident to us than when we are the center of attention, when we can see all those eyes gazing directly upon us. It is very natural, then, for our pulse to quicken, our muscles to tighten, and our entire nervous system to be rapidly aroused. This reaction is a fundamental part of our human condition.

If you have frequently been up in front of others, this increased arousal will channel easily into an enthusiastic and natural level of behavior.

It will give you your "edge." But if you are not experienced in speaking before others—and most people, even many executives, are not—this surge of energy, especially if it is not being channeled into action, may spill over into an anxiety syndrome. Anxiety syndrome, of course, is nothing more than a high-class name for stage fright, the butterflies, or just the plain old shakes. Its symptoms run the gamut from an extreme of nausea to a mild case of dry mouth. Your muscular reactions can range from a tight voice to shaking knees. The outward signs can be anything from a glassy stare to pulling at your collar. Your worst fear is passing out entirely and making an absolute fool of yourself. The usual consequences are that you are uncomfortable, but you live through it. And what not enough anxious speakers know is that you seldom appear as nervous to others as you may feel to yourself.

The good news is that virtually all of us can rid ourselves of the negative consequences of anxiety over getting up in front of others. Churchill did it; so did Lincoln and John F. Kennedy. Scores of professional entertainers surprise readers of their autobiographies by revealing how absolutely petrified they have been in front of vast audiences— especially on opening night.

Consider the case of Roger H. If he could do it, so can you.

By day Roger was a junior accountant, and by night he put in long hours finishing up a degree, a task no doubt hampered by his being a severe stutterer. Although completion of one speech course was a requirement for his degree plan, Roger had been told that he could waive it on the grounds of being "handicapped." This had so enraged him that he took completion of the course as a near life-or-death challenge. In those first few meetings when students introduce themselves, Roger got by with a labored word or two, mostly with the effect that both he and the class dreaded the night when it came time for his first major presentation.

That night came, and Roger moved to the lectern before an absolutely hushed group. He was visibly sweating through an obviously new suit. His hands shook so violently that he nearly toppled a stand upon which he had placed a chart to supplement his speech on spiders. He seemed too shaken to distribute the four or five live specimens he had in clear plastic boxes.

In the first minute, he was able only to stammer a greeting and repeat his name. The entire second minute dragged by before he could get past the first few words of his opening sentence. The third minute passed without a word. In the fourth minute, Roger put his hands to his face as his knees buckled. A young woman in the front row murmured, "Oh no . . ." Another thirty seconds passed.

Then, with a deliberateness that must have drawn upon every fiber in his body, Roger slowly gave his talk—at first behind his hands, then later facing his listeners, and eventually moving among them as he passed out the plastic boxes. At the fifteenth minute, Roger concluded on schedule. With the same calculated deliberateness and effort, he asked if there were any questions. Just to be sure that Roger was not left in the lurch by a totally exhausted class, I offered the question. Holding up a box containing an agitated spider, I asked: "What's that sound he's making?"

"I . . . I . . It's a . . a . . a sh . . sh . . she," he responded. "I . . I . . it m . . means sh . . sh . . she's sexually excited!"

That marked the end of the first and the last speech of the evening. Nothing else was possible.

So maybe even Churchill had his problems with stage fright, but Roger H. stands out the most to me as proof that anybody with courage and persistence, no matter the odds, can rise to the occasion!

Three Steps to Confident Speech

If you will take the next ten to fifteen minutes and study three simple steps, then have the persistence to apply them, the odds are that you can substantially reduce your anxieties about getting up in front of others. The odds are good in your favor, too, that the same energy that feeds your feelings of nervousness can be channeled into confidence and enthusiasm. Try them.

> Step One: Plan as if your life depended on it.
> Step Two: Get rid of last-minute butterflies.
> Step Three: Transform anxiety into excitement.

Step One: Plan as if Your Life Depended on It

If you are an especially alert person, greatly concerned with doing well, and perhaps inexperienced at public speaking, you will be prone to stage fright. But you also are well equipped to do something about it. There are ways to lessen your overall anxiety about a forthcoming speech. There are also ways to "valve off" the symptoms of stage fright when they do strike. Mostly, you will want to maintain a fair degree of arousal, but you will want to channel it into your communication power. If you research, plan, and rehearse your speech to the point where you are highly confident of the content, this confidence will begin to overshadow stage fright.

> Plan more than you think necessary for your basic message, so that you feel well backed up with information. Have a file of facts or data on hand for further reference. Make your final speech materials the tip of the iceberg—your "blue chip" material.
>
> Imagine your listener in a one-on-one conversation with you as you practice your speech. Set your notes out on a table or bulletin board and talk through them conversationally to yourself, to a tape recorder, or to anybody who will

listen to you. As you do this, bear in mind that in our modern times, some of the most effective styles of public speaking are like enlarged conversation. Silver-tongued oratory is out.

If you are really worried about going blank, write out a script to keep handy, then quit worrying about it.

If your presentation could be the break that you have been looking for, pull out all the stops for preparation. Rehearse your speech with a professional (look for one in any nearby university or consulting agency). Consider having a videotape made, then evaluate the results with a professional. (It never ceases to amaze me how some executives who have their careers and their company's dollars on the line fail to give a crucial presentation the hours of preparation it deserves.) What is your presentation worth? Are you investing enough in it?

Step Two: Get Rid
of Last-Minute Butterflies

There are tried-and-true methods for lessening tension in the period immediately before the speech. Some of them should work well for you.

Dress in whatever makes you feel especially confident. Often this will be just slightly more formal than the dress of your audience. (The last thing you want to worry about is how you look.)

Plan your arrival for the speech so there is absolutely no chance for last-minute crises of being late, finding the room, or getting the lights on. Any of these problems can stir up your anxiety to unnecessary levels.

Examine the room where you will be speaking. Get familiar with it so you will not have any surprises (e.g., how you enter and exit, type of lectern, lighting, possible furniture rearrangements). Walk around in the room. See what it's like to sit in the audience. If you have the opportunity, give your talk a run-through. Pick out two or three features (paintings, light fixtures, ceiling decor, etc.) that you like about the room—features that make you feel good. Expect to feel comfortable when you see them during your speech.

Arrive early enough so you can meet some of your audience. Chat with them informally about your topic. Your speech simply will be an enlargement of this. Conversations will get you into a communicative attitude. Also, people whom you meet before a speech will often give you positive feedback (eye contact, smiles) when you are making your presentation. Meeting audience members as they arrive is sometimes very effective if the group is not too large (e.g., under fifty). (Use memory association techniques—Chapter 20—to remember a few names. Then make a personal reference or two during your speech.)

If you find physical tension building (heart pounding, fast breathing, shaking), either just prior to or during your speech, valve it into physical action. Move around. (Locked knees will shake; bent ones being flexed will not.) Stretch your hands and arms. (Don't lock your arms in front of you or go "white knuckles" on the lectern. Instead, move your hands and arms for gestures. Rub your hands together once or twice.) Before the speech, a little deep breathing (big breath in, let out slowly, maybe even with counting) can get your breath under control. (Yes, it's like the natural childbirth technique, and it works!)

Step Three: Transform
Anxiety Into Excitement

Usually you will be more nervous just before delivering your speech than you will be once you finally get started. There are techniques for insuring a smooth start and for handling stage fright once you are on.

> Remember as you speak that arousal can look as much like excitement and enthusiasm to an audience as it seems like anxiety to you. Don't worry if you appear worked up.
>
> Have an introduction written out to give beforehand to the person who will introduce you. This will alleviate sometimes embarrassing or amateurish introductions which might bother you.
>
> Have a fail-safe introduction for your presentation, something you know for sure will work. A speech does not have to start with a joke, but if you start with material that guarantees some positive audience feedback, that response will put you on your way to winning.
>
> If you wish, acknowledge to your audience that you are worked up over your presentation. Make this a positive statement. Don't apologize. (You're "excited," not "scared silly.")

Now see if you don't feel better about getting up in front of others. You'll enjoy it and they will too!

9

Handling Intimidation

An intimidator wants to set you up for a loss. It's a "you lose, they win" strategy. Often it's a case of negative persuasion—"Do it or else!" If you are trapped, it is often too late to do much about it. Arguing back may only reveal how really vulnerable you are. Usually you are forced to take the loss, but you can learn some lessons from it. The best way to handle intimidation is to be able to see it coming. If you know some of the devices intimidators use, you'll be able to avoid being trapped before it's too late.

HOW ABOUT "WINNING THROUGH INTIMIDATION"?

Despite Robert Ringer's best-selling book by that title, winning through intimidation is not only a negative approach to human relations, but it often backfires.

Enter "Gentleman Jim" . . .

Jim was one of four project officers for a multimillion-dollar nonprofit foundation founded by a prestigious living family. His job was to serve a liaison role between individuals or organizations and the foundation, which had sponsored their projects. Jim was a good "front man"—good-looking, well-dressed, with a truly engaging personality. People felt good around him—at least at first. He could make you feel as if your work was the most important project the foundation had going. To many, Jim was "Gentleman Jim."

As a consequence, Jim's clients would confide in him, sometimes sharing very personal thoughts or disclosures about their organizations. Little did his clients know that Jim kept as meticulous notes about such inside information on people and organizations as he did on the projects he was paid to oversee. This was Jim's strategy (or as one victim said, his "ammunition") for staying one up on individuals who could make him vulnerable. Jim was no gentleman at all.

When a misunderstanding or disagreement did develop between the foundation and the director of a project, Jim used his "ammunition" to defend his position. In one case, when roughly ten thousand dollars had been spent on a book that did not materialize on schedule, Jim hinted to the foundation about the author's apparent "drug problem." The author not only lost his grant but his part-time teaching position as well. In another case, when a project director resisted Jim's second request to pay a large bill for him at a local luxury hotel, Jim countered by threatening to reveal the director as a closet homosexual.

Jim got away with his intimidation strategies for almost three years, until an apparent opportunity was turned into a nightmare. The foundation's president invited Jim and three of their most brilliant former clients to form a committee to write a "white paper" on new funding priorities. Two of the clients declined, tactfully telling the president of their negative experiences with Jim.

When the president, who could not fully believe the accusations, asked Jim about the two individuals, Jim's response was to allude to one individual's "live-in girl friend" and the other's budgetary disagreement with a government funding agency. Then, as the president began to describe the nature of the allegations, he found Jim alluding to the bad publicity that might result if the newspapers found out about the types of individuals the foundation had been supporting.

Jim was given a one-month termination notice and asked to vacate his office that day. (And the president felt relieved that he had never gotten to know Jim personally!)

Intimidation is not only a deceitful approach to human relations, it is simply bad business—especially if you want to do repeat business.

Looking Out for Intimidators

Despite our disagreement about winning through intimidation, Robert Ringer does give some good advice in his book when he describes three types of intimidators. Our "Gentleman Jim" is the type who disarms you with charm while loading up on his own ammunition. This person is the most devious, the most deceitful of the intimidators. Personal interest and charm are used as a ploy to get information or to disarm your suspicion of being intimidated.

> Beware of the overly engaging individual who shares inside information with you. He may just as well be sharing your information with another person. He is busy putting you in a "loss" position in case he needs it. Look out for the person who uses intimidation as a way of life, but tries to hide it from you until the kill. This intimidator is the wolf in sheep's clothing.

There is also the intimidator who starts off a relationship with all good intentions, but when the going gets rough, will use anything to win. (How about calling him "End-Run Jim"?) This is the individual who will make an "end run" or go for the "zero-sum game" (they win a point, you lose it). This is the "Sorry, Harvey, it's either you or me," or "I really hate doing this but I have no choice," or "I'm forced into it" type of person. These intimidators are not necessarily clever or charming. They are often weak individuals.

> Watch for individuals who seem honest but who would not be above taking a win at your expense if they saw an opportunity to do so. Beware of the person who has a record of trying to cash in on others, who will turn a "you win, I win" situation into a "you lose, I win" game if the opportunity presents itself.

The third type of intimidators, the most blatant, may actually be the least dangerous to you because you can easily spot and avoid them. This is "Head On Jim," with his "it's either you or me" attitude in the situation. This person is competitive rather than deceitful. But nonetheless, the strategy is still intimidation; and most of us, if we are smart, will choose to avoid "you lose, I win" games—even if we win them from time to time.

> When confronted by an outright intimidator, ask yourself if there is not some strategy to change the situation to one of "both win" rather than "one wins, one loses." Better yet, steer clear of even the above-board intimidator. Even if you win, it may not be worth it in the long run.

Eight Kinds of Communications That Are Out to Get You

All of us at one time or another fall prey to ploys in communication. These may or may not be part of an overall intimidation strategy, but they are set up to make us lose. Watch out for them.

1. Super Strokes
("Gee, you really owe it to yourself.")
We all like compliments. We all like to be winners. Super strokes are used to get people so flattered, feeling good, or thinking about doing something for themselves that they overlook more important parts of an argument.

> Look out for "strokes" as a bargaining ploy. You get the compliments while the other person gets the win. Beware when strokes are used early in negotiation, especially when the other person is not a close friend, and when compliments or statements directed to your self-interest are emphasized. Acknowledge them, but get back down to relevant details of your interaction.

2. Personal Put-Downs
("You don't get it and never will!")

As we emphasized in Chapter 3, attacking people instead of problems usually just creates more problems. This is argument "to the person," where the attempt is to substitute personal attack for a logical approach to the issues at hand. ("You're all wrong on this, Sally. The figures couldn't be that bad!") Sometimes the attack comes in the form of sarcasm. ("Helen, did you do that draft on your kid's typewriter?")

> Watch for arguments that are directed to you as a person rather than to the logical details of the discussion. Separate people from their arguments. If somebody tries to attack you personally in an argument, ask for a chance to stand back "so we can review the issues." If sarcasm is becoming too heavy in your dealings with another person, ask tactfully (and privately) that it be avoided in the future.

3. Logical Frauds
(". . . therefore you ought to buy it.")

Because our speech is so often a shorthand, informal version of our thoughts, the differences between logical argument and statements parading as logic sometimes slip by us.

> Whenever someone tries to lead you to a logical conclusion, especially implicitly (for example, by saying "therefore"), test the logic. Or else look out for some common ploys and fallacies. Review the logical sequence with the person if you think that it is worth it.

Have you come across any of the following "logical" ploys or outright fallacies?

"You know, most of what that company puts out is nothing but trash. We're buying their subassemblies and that really disappoints me." (Looks like a logical sequence but it is a well-known fallacy. *Most* doesn't mean *all.*)

"If you use our small computer system, chances are that it will cut your accounting costs in half. It happened to us." (Typical kind of product endorsement cleverly worded to avoid a Federal Trade Commission crackdown. It guarantees nothing.)

"Whenever I'm out of the shop for a day, something breaks down. I'm tired of this staff being so careless with our equipment." (Could be coincidence. Correlation does not prove cause and effect.)

"The phone company hit a market low yesterday; computer companies are up, *therefore* I suggest you buy. . . ." (Look out for *therefore.* Its use can make almost anything sound logical.)

"Nine out of ten managers can't tell the difference between a computer-generated letter and a hand-typed one." (Illusion of scientific testing. Forget it unless they have conducted an objective study.)

"I can personally assure you that if you install our pumps, your maintenance will go down two hundred percent." (Opinion parading as fact. A verbal guarantee won't get far in court if you sue for nonperformance.)

4. Bandwagon Ploy
("Go ahead, everybody's doing it.")
Everybody might not be doing it. Or everybody might be wrong.

"Bandwagon" is often a sales ploy, especially if coupled with the further warning that "if you don't buy now, there might not be any left." None of us wants to be left behind, but beware when "bandwagon" is used as a primary argument or as a closing ploy to get you to make your decision. Even if everybody is actually doing it, does it really make any difference to you?

5. The Big Shot
("Look, I've been here fifteen years, I ought to know.")
The Big Shot throws his weight around; he intimidates by being overbearing.

Although supervisor-subordinate distinctions are a fact of organizational life, beware of following the Big Shot blindly. Look for reasons for following or declining. The Big Shot ploy is a substitute for genuine leadership capabilities. It also creates an unproductive, hostile work environment. If the situation looks too permanent to you, get out before the Big Shot leads you, the others, and himself out.

6. Garden-Hose Views
("Just look at it my way.")
Some people can only see things in their own narrow, tunnel-vision way. It's easier for them to force others to their point of view than to try to see alternatives.

Watch out for individuals who pressure you to view a situation only their way. Their real grounds for the argument may be that they cannot see things any other way. Try to discuss alternatives, not as a challenge to their view, but simply as a report of your views. Ask for outside advice; get it in writing.

7. Guilt Trip
("Don't you think you owe some allegiance to a company that gave you your first management experience?")
A guilt trip is often a last-ditch ploy. It is increasingly meaningless to employees in growth industries who may have more allegiance to their profession and life-style than to a particular company.

When you get a guilt trip disguised as an argument, look especially carefully for other reasons for your decision or action. Allegiance has merit, yes, but you ought to be clear about it if the other person thinks that's an effective tactic to motivate you. (Maybe it's not as important to you as they think.) Also, allegiance can be the basis for positive motivation (the company wins, you win) rather than as a negative guilt appeal.

8. Happy Deception
("Why not believe it anyway?")
Sometimes we are so anxious for a win that we will believe anything.

Ruth B., after being passed over for promotion to higher-level management after four years, spent two more years as a clerical supervisor in an insurance firm because her boss consistently told her that she had "management potential." In reality, it was the only positive thing he could think of to say during the three semiannual promotion interviews where he had to break the news of her turndown. The problem was that Ruth wanted to believe the positive parts of what he said even though the facts were otherwise.

Be on guard against self-deception. Test the facts of the situation with anyone who is a good enough friend to listen to you but sufficiently objective to see through any happy deception. Test your interpretations of possibly deceptive statements by asking questions. Get the other person to make the implicit explicit. Ask for answers in writing.

COMPLIANCE VERSUS CONFLICT RESOLUTION

In modern theories of negotiation, a distinction is made between trying to get another person to believe or do exactly as you want (compliance) and working together to negotiate a mutually desirable outcome (conflict resolution). Compliance is the norm in many everyday types of business and organizational communications. However, if a disagreement or misunderstanding arises, and no opportunity is offered for conflict resolution, intimidation is almost the inevitable result. This forces a loss on either you or the other party, instead of the possibility of mutual wins.

Mutual wins build a positive working relationship based on trust. They set the stage for further and higher risk (and reward) "you win, I win" games.

Forced compliance through intimidation, although you or the other person may score a unilateral win, also mandates a loss. Losses promote a negative working environment. Individuals will avoid situations and people associated with earlier losses, or else they will try intimidation tactics such as revenge. Sooner or later, as in the case of "Gentleman Jim," consistent intimidators have to face up to the losses they have perpetrated.

10

Avoiding
Information Overload

Does just the thought of reading or listening make you tired? Are you missing important points too often in your business communications? Do you have to either stay late or take papers home if you hope to keep up with it all? Does a ringing telephone jangle your nerves (even at home)? This malady is information overload, and it's an increasingly prevalent problem in today's information-crammed offices. Too often we show all the symptoms of overload before we think of doing something about it. Know how to see it coming. Plan ways to avoid it. Use the four steps of communications time management.

"HARRY HARD DRIVEN"

Harry D. was thirty-five and trying hard to launch himself into middle management. He supervised fifteen salespersons and an office staff of five in the power tool division of a $500 million manufacturing firm. Harry displayed all of the trappings of the hard-driven executive. By 10:30 A.M. his tie was at half-mast, he was predictably a half hour behind on his appointments, and he was on his fifth cup of coffee. Lunch was usually a sandwich sent in and consumed over an increasingly disordered and paper-stacked desk. Harry was often the last to leave at night; and when he left, he carried a briefcase full of papers. He was not reluctant to tell his co-workers how overloaded he was.

Harry used his work load as an explanation for why he missed deadlines, made occasional errors in sales estimates, and did not return important calls promptly. He occasionally missed important information in incoming correspondence, and sometimes had to plead with his staff to put in extra time to help him catch up (which he never did).

Despite his problems, the staff acknowledged that nobody seemed to work as hard as "Harry Hard Driven," a name coined by an executive intern in the next office.

Nor did anybody work as inefficiently.

When Harry got his transfer, it was to a comparable-level position in another division, not to middle management, which surprised some of the office staff because he seemed to work so hard. But after about a month, they learned why. Harry's replacement, Phil S., was able to assume all of Harry's duties, but without the hard-driven executive image. Moreover, Phil made far fewer mistakes.

The story of Harry illustrates most of the symptoms of information overload, a term becoming increasingly popular in the modern organizational world. It also illustrates the major reason this problem is so often more associated with a particular person than a particular job. It is typically a personal problem of communications time management. And its usual cure is to employ better methods for handling the deluge of information that floods our modern offices.

Four Strategies for Combating Information Overload

Because these strategies assume that the common cause of the overload lies in inefficient use of communications time, be certain first that there is no other major reason for your problems. For example, are you in reasonably good physical and mental health? Nothing in the four strategies will be of much help to persons who simply do not have the energy required for a heavy work load, or who are too worn down to take assertive control of their daily schedules. It can also be possible that your position in an organization has grown too burdensome for one person to carry. Perhaps a recent reorganization or new project has created an overload situation. Several of the following strategies will help you to identify the latter cause.

However, for the vast majority of information overload situations, either occasional or chronic, better communications time management is the primary solution.

Begin by taking a good day's rest for yourself, then try any of the following strategies that look useful to you.

1. Review Your Responsibilities

Identify the responsibilities associated with your position. Assign priorities to them, then evaluate the relative amounts of communication time spent on each.

Write out, or sketch out in chart form, the key responsibilities of your job. Arrange them in order of importance to the organization and to yourself. Think through the types of communications you usually use to carry out these responsibilities. Jot them down. Then alongside each, note how relatively time-consuming these communications are (e.g., H = heavy, M = moderate, L = light, and N = negligible). Don't bother calculating actual amounts of time or making a detailed time analysis. (You don't have time!)

Next, evaluate how levels of time consumption correlate with your priority rankings. Look especially for mismatches—i.e., heavy amounts of time spent on low-priority activities, or perhaps negligible or small amounts of time spent on activities that could use more of your attention.

Sometimes the above strategy alone can solve your problem. For example, you might be spending several hours a week in meetings with the company's personnel committee, although you have no responsibilities for personnel. Or you might notice that time you have spent on crisis-laden low-priority items has kept you away from important responsibilities. (The two hours spent meeting personally with two feuding secretaries could better have been spent in further refining your upcoming presentation to the directors.)

In short, actively shift your communications time allocations according to priorities you have assigned to your responsibilities.

Do you truly have more communications requirements than you can possibly handle? Has your position gotten overburdened? If so, take the facts to upper management to see if you can have changes made. (Presenting the facts about the tasks without referring to your personal problems of time will be persuasive.)

Has change or reorganization resulted in your overloading an office under you? Are you trading off your overload problems to another office or person? Again, use the facts to convince upper management to realign responsibilities.

2. Cut Your Information Flow

Examine where you can cut or reduce time-consuming communications activities. Keep your position responsibilities and priorities in mind.

Cut some of the bulk out of your incoming correspondence and documents. Have your secretary screen incoming mail more tightly, putting very low priority items in a reading file that you may (or may not) get to later. Have your secretary handle responses to routine correspondence. Delegate correspondence and other paperwork as much as possible. (See Chapter 18 for more ideas.)

Develop a priority system for having your telephone calls screened. Set criteria for when you should be interrupted to take an incoming call. Have efficient methods for having phone messages taken for you. (See Chapter 13 for more details.)

Set criteria for scheduling face-to-face meetings. (Is it important enough to merit your valuable personal time?) Will a telephone call (or teleconference) handle it? Can you delegate responsibility so another person can meet the individual? Have you gotten advance information so you are sure that the meeting is worth it or so you do not have to spend face-to-face time getting background? Set definite and workable limits upon the amount of time scheduled. (Remember your responsibility priorities.)

Evaluate the importance of meetings to you. Is it important that you attend in person? Could the minutes be sent to you instead? Could you call a participant for whatever information is important to you?

All of these suggestions require the cooperation of staff in saving your valuable communications time. Training them may seem time-consuming and expensive at first, but the ultimate results will be time savings for your schedule. Remember, too, that face-to-face and group meetings take some of the control of your time out of your hands, so schedule them especially carefully.

3. Use Efficiency Tactics

It is not difficult to reduce the time typically spent on most communications activities.

> Do you vary your reading speed so as to get what you need from a letter, document, or report in the least amount of time? (Try the executive speed-reading techniques described in Chapter 18.)
>
> As a listener, realize that you can listen at a rate two to three times faster than the other person can speak to you. Do you use this advantage over the speaker in order to evaluate what you hear and to plan your responses? (See Chapter 17.)
>
> Are you using memory strategies so you do not have to spend repeated time looking up information, names, dates, or numbers? (See Chapter 20.)
>
> Are you writing or typing when you could be dictating?
>
> Can a short personal note from you replace the time and expense of a formal letter? Will a phone call do it?
>
> If you must skim periodicals or technical publications, get an agreement among your colleagues to share the load.
>
> Do you read too much mail twice—once when skimming the incoming batch, then once when you are acting on it? Don't. Handle the easy items immediately upon the first skimming (read with your dictation machine in hand).
>
> Look out for office mates who come by to discuss problems which have no bearing on your work and will take up large chunks of conversation time.
>
> Do you know how to wind up a telephone conversation when you have fulfilled your purpose? (See Chapter 13.)

4. Take Charge
of Your Personal
Communications Schedule

Too often we let others take charge of our personal communications time. We sit through meetings, not all of which pertain to us. We listen patiently while a speaker may ramble on, possibly never making the point that interests us. Our personal as well as business mailboxes are dumping grounds. Telephone calls of the most trivial nature break into our important work activities.

People often take our time as if it were an inexpensive commodity. Quite the contrary—time is among your most precious assets, so protect it!

> After you have cut as much trivia as possible from your communications activities, set up a general schedule for daily tasks. Adapt the schedule to your

personal efficiency cycle. Save your most alert hours for high-priority items. This is the period for your greatest creativity. Allocate it carefully. Because routine items tend to involve habitual rather than creative activities, save them for your periods of lower efficiency. Set up reliable barriers against interruptions—especially telephone calls—during your peak efficiency periods.

Although much advice is often given as to what to do first each day or when your "peak" periods occur, figuring out your personal schedule rather than following some standard one will pay the most dividends. Some of us are morning people; others are afternoon people. Make your own best balance between your organization's needs and your daily cycle. Then set the pace of your work accordingly.

Group together tasks that require a common type of work. For example, if you can set aside your routine telephone callbacks, make yourself comfortable (maybe using an earphone set if you have many calls to make), then make all of your calls at a common time. Pick one time of the day to read your incoming mail. Try to establish routines that reduce as much as possible reading letters twice. Answer the routine items as you read them (preferably with your dictating equipment in hand). If at all possible, group together appointments that are not of high priority; keep them brief. (The next appointment showing up is the easiest reason to conclude the current one.)

Obviously you cannot always keep to the desired schedule. But if you get a schedule going, the time saved will be available to handle crises and rush jobs.

Plan to use your "dead time" more efficiently. Keep a few tasks handy in your briefcase so you can get a start on them if you find yourself waiting an extra half hour in your dentist's office. Keep a few items to work on in the back of your mind during dull periods in a long meeting. Most of us already do work while traveling by air or train, but have you thought about ways to use audio tapes while driving? Dictation of simple items is not difficult while on the freeway (but don't sail past your off ramp!). You or your associates can make audio tape briefings which you can play back while driving to that important meeting.

The point is not to make yourself busy every moment of your waking day, but to take advantage of spare time if you wish to. If you haven't planned ahead, you have no choice.

Look out for old habits in planning your personal communications schedule. For example, don't assume that you should start the day by reading your mail. Don't assume that you should go to every meeting to which you are invited (get the minutes). Double-check every communications activity to be sure you are not slipping into old habits.

Expect crises or rush projects to be a regular part of your schedule. Don't make your schedule so rigid that a change will make you feel you have lost control.

The more responsibilities you have, the more you may have to adapt to important interruptions. As an executive, you may often have to handle high-priority tasks that are nonroutine. Therefore, expect to be flexible in your personal work schedule. Plan for it, and the unexpected or the rush job will not bog you down. But when a rush job does come up, be frank with yourself. Can you really get it done? Is it sufficiently important? If other tasks will suffer, be frank with those who are depending upon you. Learn to say no when necessary (if you are in a position to do so).

> Aggressively plan time for rest and respite. Avoid constantly cutting into your lunch hour with overload business. Eventually your efficiency may drop to the point where you are actually losing time by overworking. Plan a break or two during the day to clear your mind, then take stock of how the day is going.

Know not only your daily cycle and adjust your pace to it, but look more broadly at your weekly or even monthly cycles. This will pay dividends for longer-range communications activities (e.g., report writing). It will allow you to set overall schedules and interim deadlines.

Best yet, a broader view of your schedule will allow you to review your overall progress in your communications time management program.

And remember, too, that the constantly rushed executive, the one with the impossible work load who feels he's so important that he works weekends and skips vacations, is often demonstrating his lack of effective planning rather than dedication and hard work!

11

Interviewing

Unless our job requires daily interviewing, we often take the process of interviewing too much for granted. The greatest problem with interviews is due to the lack of planning on the part of the interviewer. The most effective interview is purpose-oriented. How you conduct it may vary greatly according to whether the purpose is decision making, planning, appraisal or evaluation, reprimand, firing, praise, information giving or gathering, or handling complaints. Use a proposed three-step process for interviewing, which will get you results. Also think about turning the tables. What if you're the one being interviewed?

ALL IN A DAY

Marsha G., an absolutely first rate student in our communications management program, had the good fortune to be interviewed for three jobs in the same day. One was with a cable TV company, the second with a network-owned local TV station, and the third in the industrial communications department of a major oil company. When she came by for coffee the next morning, I was anxious to hear how her interviews had gone.

"I'm sure glad that I had some better times yesterday after the morning's disaster," sighed Marsha, clearly ready to share her experiences with me. "The guy in the cable company hardly gave me a chance to talk. When I did get in a few words about banking services over the cable, he told me they weren't in that business and never would be. It was like all he wanted to do was to prove to me that he knew everything about the cable business and I was an idiot. He didn't even have the résumé that I had sent."

"The TV station visit made me feel better. The personnel director did the interviewing. She had read my résumé and right off made me feel like a professional. We

could have gotten a really good conversation going, but her phone kept interrupting us. After this happened about three times, I got the feeling that she was now more concerned with some crisis than with what I was telling her. They are having me in for a callback, however," added Marsha, wanting to be more positive about the interview.

"My biggest surprise was the oil company. I didn't think that they would be all that interested in me," explained Marsha, *setting the stage for what had obviously turned out to be the best interview of the day. "First off, the communications director met with me personally. When I was expecting him to grill me on what I knew about corporate video, he asked me about my summer in Sweden. I think that he was personally interested in Swedish TV. It was only in the last few minutes that he asked me about my ideas for what's next in uses for videotape and disc in business. I laid out a five-minute overview and also promised to send him the case-study paper I did in seminar last fall."*

"After all my talk about getting ahead in entertainment TV, I'll be more surprised than you to be working in the oil business," quipped an obviously happy Marsha.

I know Marsha well enough to just about guarantee that she would be a smashing success in any of the three jobs. The important point is not so much Marsha's disappointment with the first two interviews, but the fact that those companies missed their chances to gain an outstanding employee. The cable-TV interviewer was obviously inexperienced and probably fed his insecurities by preying on job applicants. The TV station personnel officer was no doubt skilled as an interviewer, but either she or her office couldn't control interruptions, the bane of a successful interview. The communications director at the oil company got his money's worth from a personally oriented and highly effective interview.

And he got his company a first-rate young executive.

BE CLEAR ON YOUR PURPOSES FOR THE INTERVIEW

Too often managers mistakenly consider "to interview" as one of the general purposes for which we use face-to-face communication in organizations. Sure, interviewing is a type of communication, but it has varied purposes which will affect how you do the job. The failure to sense these varied purposes, and particularly to plan with purpose, is a major cause of failure in interviewing.

Here are some brief notes on interview purposes and their respective planning implications.

Decision Making, Planning

This interview is a key to participatory management. When you get other people actively involved in planning, they develop a more positive commitment to carrying out the plan. In such interviews you probably know the individual well, so you do not need time to get adjusted to each other before getting down to business. You can ask for a decision plan to be submitted to you before the meeting. In these interviews, give the person you are meeting with maximum lead time; make it clear that the objective is to get the decision or plan made at the time of the meeting.

Appraisal, Evaluation, or Praise

These interviews should have a maximum lead time, including the possibility of long-range scheduling (e.g., every quarter). An exception is to schedule a commendation interview as close as possible to the performance of that act. For appraisal and evaluation, an important planning priority is to create a positive and supportive attitude about the interview. Don't let your appraisal interviews become known as witch hunts or third-degree sessions. Get individuals into a mode of self-evaluation, of summarizing job requirements, then review their achievements. Stress a "we" attitude in seeking improvements in performance rather than pinning the other person down with "why's" about problems. Have the performance summary submitted in advance of your interview, then use the valuable face-to-face time to concentrate on priority items.

Reprimand and Firing

These interviews are usually best scheduled with a very short lead time. If you tell Sally on Thursday that you want to meet with her next Monday about her poor performance, you'll be setting up a no-win stress situation. Although the meeting may be best on short notice, don't fail to give yourself time to be sure of your objectives. If an immediate reprimand is deserved from some incident you've discovered, give yourself time to get the facts and perhaps to cool off. In our modern era of job rights, unions, and federal regulations, be sure you know where you stand legally with a firing. (For example, do you have a record of written warnings to back you up?) Although you may feel like giving a fired person a real dressing down, consider the likely costs to you (like a lawsuit). Your purpose is to remove the employee from your organization, not to get all your complaints aired.

Information Giving or Getting

These interviews are usually scheduled on a short-range basis as the need arises. It is most important to be clear about what you want. Consider preceding the interview with a written report so the meeting can concentrate on the most important points or can be used for clarification of feedback.

Hiring

"Qualify" the candidate before obligating yourself or others for interview time. Study the résumé. Make a few phone calls to references and to prior employers (especially if they are not given also as references). Consider who else the individual should meet during the visit. Will you want to have some material for the candidate to take home? Have a meeting environment that is pleasant and not intimidating (maybe a meeting room rather than an office). Consider sending materials for the person to examine prior to the interview. (See if he or she takes the initiative to study it.) Plan on an opening question or two that will put the candidate at ease (hobbies, travel, schools).

Complaints

Often these will come from employees who feel that they have been mistreated by others, have not gotten the raise or promotion they sought, or have some resentment that has been building in them. The greatest problem with these interviews is that you can be caught unprepared. The other person has done much more thinking as well as gotten very emotionally involved. You'll do best when you know what is coming. You won't be caught by surprise and you can do some fact-finding. Above all, if you can afford the time and want to keep the employee, let the person talk it out. Often, sympathetic listening and a few constructive suggestions will set things right until you can get to the heart of the problem.

Three Steps
for Interviews That Get Results

Step One: Plan With Purpose
Schedule the interview so it is to your advantage (short notice for reprimands, long notice for information or appraisals).

Know your purpose and stick to it (maybe making a note along with the appointment). If others will also be doing interviewing (as with a job candidate), be sure they know the purpose.

Request or send out prior information as appropriate so you can focus the interview on what's important.

Consider the best setting for the interview. If it's for praise, lunch would be appropriate (and a perquisite—"perk"). You'll get to know your job candidate faster if the interview setting is pleasant.

Plan so you will not be interrupted during the interview.

Be sure you have all you need to know for your interview—information is power.

Step Two: Probe With Purpose
If you do not already know the other person and you want to insure the most positive face-to-face communication, then your first purpose will be to put the

60

other person at ease. Do this with probes that allow for pleasant, comfortable, and rewarding responses. (Again, hobbies and travel often fit into this category.)

Use questions that lead you to the purposes of the interview, but as much as possible let the other person do the talking. Use questions that cannot be answered with a simple yes or no or the name of something. ("Have you worked with die stamps before?" will likely get you only a "Yes," and you already knew this or you wouldn't be having the interview. Try "What experiences have you had with die stamps?")

Avoided loaded questions that put the other person in a bind. ("Do you think we're the best company in the market?")

Where you wish, use brief open-ended questions that will prompt elaboration. ("How did that system work?")

If you are getting more details than you want on a topic, feel free to shift the subject. The interviewee will usually be trying to tell you what you are interested in hearing, so it is your responsibility to make clear what you want.

If the other person has obviously misunderstood your question, allow a chance to try again. ("That's not exactly what I meant. Let me put it this way. . . .")

Give plenty of feedback—both verbal ("Yes," "OK," "Uh-huh," "Good") and nonverbal (nods, smiles, eye contact)—while the other person talks.

Again, cut interruptions to a minimum.

Use listening strategies (see Chapter 17) for using your time advantage over the speaker to evaluate what you hear. Read nonverbal cues (eye contact, gestures, facial expression, mannerisms) which may tell you about confidence, honesty, interest, and other emotional reactions.

Step Three:
Follow up With Purpose

Decide on the next step at the conclusion of the interview. Make it clear what you want the person to do, if anything. Any effective interview should move you to the next square (even if it is deciding that you don't want the person for the job).

Make notes on the results, if they will be of use to you or anybody else. One of the most effective tactics you can use to help your personnel department is to always follow up an employment interview with a note to them.

Are follow-up memos always necessary? Face-to-face meetings are excellent for personal motivation, but they leave no record unless you make one. If you want action, write a follow-up memo—one copy for the record and one for the person to do the action.

IF YOU ARE BEING INTERVIEWED

You can easily draw your own pointers from the materials in the previous section if you are the one to be interviewed. Above all, ask yourself these questions:

1. What is my personal purpose in the interview? How does it fit the purpose of the other person, or what must I do to make the best compromise?

2. Do I have all possible information that will be valuable to me for the interview? (This may be obvious if you are told to furnish certain information. But, for example, for an employment interview, have you studied the company's annual report or looked for articles on it in the local or a business newspaper?) What do I know about the person interviewing me? How can I find out more?

3. Am I minimizing all possible chances for slipups that could damage my effectiveness? (It still amazes me that people are so often late for an employment interview and feel that the excuse of confusing directions or heavy traffic will suffice. Why not make a trial run the day before? Or go an hour early and relax over a cup of coffee at a nearby café?)

4. What questions can I anticipate? (Always be ready for that personal, "off guard" question. It's meant to reveal how you will react to something unexpected.) If I do not have answers for some questions, can I furnish good reasons why?

5. Am I dressed and groomed properly for the interview? (Despite the seeming triviality of this point, managers will refer time and time again to dress and grooming in their informal remarks about a job applicant.) Pay an anonymous visit to the organization; see how the employees dress. Then go just a step—a tiny one—better for the interview.

12

Winning the
Meetings Game

Most meetings do not work very well, so if you have been baffled, frustrated, or bored at them, that's almost the norm. Yet we can expect even more meetings as modern management takes on a more participatory form. A good meeting gets the job done, but too often it's not clear what the job is. Most meetings lack skillful "participationship" as well as leadership. There are strategies for effective participation, including how to come out ahead when you have to sit out a boring meeting. Leadership doesn't mean dominating everybody, but rather balancing discussion between getting people to put their ideas on the table and quickly synthesizing these ideas into single solutions.

"I COULDN'T BELIEVE IT!"

Sally A., a family friend, had been in her first job as a systems analyst for about eight months when we had the chance to lunch together and to talk over her first experiences on the job. As expected, Sally was doing very well. She had even gotten a merit raise after her first six months.

"It has all been terrific," said Sally. "I love my work. Everybody is so helpful. I think in about one hour everybody got over the idea that I was the first woman analyst they had hired. But there's just one thing. . . ."

"Yes," I responded, thinking that we were about to embark on a discussion of women in management.

"The meetings . . . they're such a bore! Frank, the section manager, rambles on and on. When he asks for questions, nobody says anything because all they can think of is getting out of there. Harry, who is about to retire, actually nods off for most of the meeting. Honestly, the meetings have all of the makings of a great TV skit. And I told Frank that right in front of everybody!"

"I couldn't believe it!"

It's truly unfortunate that meetings have such a bad reputation. They have all of the potential to be one of the richest forms of human contact. Meetings allow us to share and to combine strategies for problem solving. They are the cornerstone of participatory management strategies. Meetings can build group commitment to an organization. Best of all for us as individuals, a successful meeting can provide a wide range of psychological and social rewards.

Why, then, do people have such a negative view of meetings? Mainly, it's because most meetings are poorly organized and conducted. They are a very complex form of communication that is taken too lightly. Too many of us sit out meetings where the leader and the group may have conflicting purposes. We are asked to respond to decisions that we know are already made. Or we are given "public" explanations of problems for which we know there are other reasons. And often we are just meeting because it is traditional to have a meeting at that time and place.

Having a successful meeting, whether you are the leader or a participant, requires a strategy. Even the best of strategies will not always guarantee positive results; for meetings, as we already warned, are complex creatures. But if you are going to meetings, or even running them, without knowing the game plan, your chances of success will be minimal.

THE POWER
OF POSITIVE PARTICIPATION

Most of us, even in managerial ranks, find ourselves sitting in meetings rather than leading them. Too often most people, unless they are scheduled to give a report, approach meetings in a passive frame of mind, as if they had no major responsibilities.

Goal Setting as a Participant

You, of course, have a responsibility to your organization or group or else you would not be meeting in the first place. But you also have a major responsibility to yourself in any meeting. What is your personal purpose, your personal goal in participation? What return do you expect on your investment of time and possibly effort?

If you are not clear on your personal goals in the meetings game, how will you know when you win?

> Try to determine the true or underlying reasons for which the meeting is being held. Do any of your reasons for attending fit these? What do you expect to give? What do you expect to get?

There are four types of purposes that reflect most reasons for holding meetings. Of course, meetings may be mixtures of these purposes. You cannot set your own goals unless you make some assumptions about the real or practical reasons for which the meeting is being held. Even though you may know the announced purpose for a meeting, it is often the subtle reasons that really count. Consider the following examples of general types of meetings as well as underlying reasons.

1. Ritual.   In one middle-sized insurance firm, the president breakfasts each Monday morning with his eleven division heads. Mostly it is a social occasion with the trappings of an executive meeting. The business parts are informal remarks by the president on topics already known to the directors. One true reason is to reaffirm personal and organizational commitment—almost like a church service. Another is to bestow a perk on the directors—a special reward for their position. Still another is to provide an informal medium for exchange of information among the directors (before and after the breakfast).

2. Informational.   Each quarter, a San Francisco publishing company brings together its forty-five regional sales representatives. They label it a management conference, but the true purpose is to review their new and upcoming books and to conduct training in sales tactics. Although the reps are invited to participate in discussions about the direction of the company and new publications, decisions in these areas are made largely by central management. The label of the meetings as well as the facade of participatory management are misleading. But in terms of these actual purposes, the meetings are highly successful.

3. Task-Oriented.   A large Eastern philanthropic foundation has an advisory board comprising experts in many areas of child development which meets annually to determine funding priorities. Like most task-oriented groups, they have a decision-making purpose for meeting which is quite clear. Yet beneath this surface are several additional important reasons for the meeting. For one, the foundation uses this annual meeting to publicly "ratify" decisions that the directors have already made. The meeting of the experts gives the whole program a stamp of approval, so to speak. Another purpose is that the staff of the foundation, who sit as "observers" at the experts' meetings as well as attend associated social functions, expand their personal contacts in the field of child development through these annual meetings.

4. Negotiation.   A midwestern construction company has a standing labor-management troubleshooting committee that meets whenever problems arise and usually when contracts are to be renewed. Although this is supposedly a jointly organized effort, it is really initiated by management as a strategy for preventing the several trade unions from getting too much of an upper hand. Management, as a meetings strategy, consistently attempts to play down differences, preferring instead to stress the "We're all one company" theme. If they were entirely successful at this—which they are not—a labor representative would almost feel rude or unfaithful to bring up the matter of more pay or better working conditions.

> Once you see where your goals and the true purposes of the meeting coincide, you are in the best possible position for positive participation. You can devote preparation time to activities that will count for your personal advancement and contribution in the meetings game. You'll be able to avoid involvements that will be a waste of your time. Best yet, you will not be wasting energy lamenting about unfulfilled expectations which were impossible in the first place.

The power of positive participation rests on your ability to identify common motives between yourself and the group. Without this knowledge, you are flying blind—and sometimes into a storm!

> If the true purposes of the meeting and your own purposes do not coincide, then seriously question why you are attending the meeting. If you are only attending because it is required or expected, then go and make the best of it. But do not set yourself up for impossible fulfillments. "Making the best of it" means that you attend in earnest, help where you can, and if nothing else, reinforce your social relationships with the others in the group.

Most of your losses at meetings consist of wasted time, boredom, or feelings of frustration. The biggest loss occurs when you vent these negative feelings in the midst of the meeting. Then nobody wins the meeting game, neither you nor the group leader. You can only avoid this disaster by sorting out your goals and the true reasons for the meeting, then figuring out a positive strategy.

Six Ways to Improve Your Participation

1. Carefully Prepare Any Presentation You May Be Called Upon to Make

Treat a meeting just like a speech. Check on the what? when? where? and how? of your presentation (see Chapter 6). Practice your presentation on a colleague. Use handouts or visual aids to get your key ideas across. Even if presentations are usually made informally, practice!

2. Use Effective Oral
and Nonverbal Delivery Tactics

Stand up if at all acceptable when you are going to address the meeting for more than a sentence or two. If possible, move to a position where you can be easily seen by all. Address the group, not just one or two members. Keep your eye contact moving.

3. Use Listening Strategies

Be sure that you hear what is said. Don't be so intent to inject your ideas that you make your contribution at the wrong moment. Use your time advantage of being able to listen faster than the other person can speak to work out your response (see Chapter 17).

4. Be Interactive

Hear the other person out before responding. Let the person who objects to your ideas say his or her piece. Don't jump in until you are sure that you have a proper response. Give others a chance to respond. Remember that sometimes no response is sufficiently effective. An efficient discussion has an idea sequence to it—an interactive pattern of idea sharing or "building." Fit your contributions into the pattern.

5. Ask for Action
When You Think You Can Get It

Sometimes a proposal is talked to death when it would have gotten enough votes to pass an hour earlier. On the other hand, if a proposal is going nowhere, move to shelve it. Don't always wait for others to make the move for action.

6. Express Positive Feelings
About the Meeting if Deserved—
Keep Negative Feelings to Yourself

Part of the "contract" for participatory management is that you will agree with the group majority even when your own ideas are rebuffed. Negative comments about a failed proposal can be taken personally by other members of the group. Positive comments build group cohesiveness and may well smooth the way for your next contributions.

HOW TO ORGANIZE AND
LEAD WINNING MEETINGS

Group leadership is an art—an optimal balance between your personality, the collective personality of the participants or the group, your shared purposes, and your leadership style. Here are six easy steps you can use to improve your meetings. You cannot expect to be an instant success as a group leader, but these steps—combined with experience—will help you to develop a winning style.

Step One: Plan With Purpose and Participants First in Mind

What precisely do you want to accomplish? Is the meeting the best way to achieve it? Do you really need to have a meeting? If so, jot down your desired outcomes. Be prepared to tell your participants what you want the group to achieve. Put that at the top of the agenda. Make your purpose their purpose.

Meetings have several distinct advantages as a communications strategy. They give you on-the-spot feedback from your colleagues. Together with your colleagues, you can develop an idea through different stages of development. You can use meetings to build group as well as individual commitment to that idea.

But remember that meetings are costly in terms of time. Also, a winning idea can get warped because discussion has been one-sided. Look out for meetings that are held simply because you usually have one at that time on that day of the week. Beware of meetings meant to talk to death an idea that no person has the individual courage to act on. Avoid especially meetings which are offered under the facade of participatory management, but where the decisions have already been made. (These damage individual commitment to an organization.)

The most successful meetings will represent a coalescence of group and individual goals. We all operate best in a group or organization where our individual goals are served by our service in the organization. Bear this truism in mind when you fit purpose and participants into your meeting plan.

Step Two: Plan the Meeting Strategy

Meeting strategies can vary between the extremes of those in which the leader virtually dictates every move to those in which leadership is widely shared among all participants. These two types are often called *leader-centered* and *group-centered* strategies.

A leader-centered strategy has a built-in efficiency of moving the meeting along rapidly. Its disadvantage is that it discourages wide participation. A group-centered strategy will often result in greater participant commitment to whatever decisions are made, but it will take more time to reach those decisions. Also, it is more difficult for a leader to impose a desired bias (if there is one) on a decision derived by a group-centered strategy.

Although many successful leaders may represent predominantly one or the other extremes in strategies, the most effective tactic is to use both.

Employ a leader-centered strategy on tasks or topics for which you do not need or desire feedback and interaction. Often these are informational items for which all you may need are questions of clarification. Ritual-type meetings are often automatically leader-centered.

Employ a group-centered strategy when you want to generate strong individual commitment to decisions and when a wide variety of alternative ideas and biases will be useful. Brainstorming meetings work best when participation is broad and individuals sense no risk in contributing the wildest of their ideas.

Consider alternating between leader- and group-centered strategies in a given meeting as the goals may fit them. In the entertainment industry, executives and creative personnel may brainstorm production ideas one day, then on the next day get down to the hard-nosed business of rigorously planning how the production will make a profit. Task-centered meetings can often benefit from a mix of strategies—group-centered to generate alternative ideas and commitment, then leader-centered to work out the action plan. Negotiation may sometimes require various mixes of strategies. Sometimes negotiations are heavily leader-centered, with one leader for each side. Other times there may be a visible attempt to demonstrate group-centeredness on the surface, yet to control with an iron hand at a deeper level.

In short, know your strategies.

Step Three: Prepare Your Agenda

Put your strategy in your agenda. You'll have more effective meetings if you think of your agenda as a game plan. How do you want the topic approached?

Suppose that your corporate accounting was falling behind due to the loss of several key exployees. You call a task-oriented meeting of key executives to propose a solution to the problem. The agenda could set up the often-used "problem-solving" sequence as follows:

1. What is the current status of our accounting problems?
2. What are our alternative solutions? (Outside help? Temporary help? Overtime? What else?)
3. What are the pros and cons of these solutions? (Costs? Time? Effects on other operations? Long-range versus short-range?)
4. Which solution to select? (We need to make that decision today!)
5. How to implement solution? (Timetable, budget, management.)

By contrast, suppose that you wanted to brainstorm new product lines in a small corporation that manufactures kitchen items. You might have the following strategic agenda for an all-day meeting:

> *8 A.M. — Meet in Upper Conference Room*
> 1. Bring to the meeting a minimum of ten new product ideas (no matter how bizarre!), each described on one sheet of paper. Make enough copies for fifteen people.
> 2. Plan to present your ideas (one minute per item) to the group.
> 3. Vote on the top five ideas.
>
> *Noon — break for lunch in Executive Dining Room*
> 4. Form a developmental team of three people each for each top idea.
> 5. Teams meet over lunch to prepare afternoon presentations for their proposed product line.
>
> *5 P.M. — Conclude*
> 6. Decide in concluding hour which product lines to send out to marketing for further study.

An action agenda isn't just a list of topics. It's your game plan!

Step Four: Anticipate the Details

The meeting room has no chalkboard. An important participant has been overlooked on the invitation list. You have twenty-five people in a room meant for fifteen. Or there are ten executives rattling around in an auditorium that seats two hundred. The microphone doesn't work. The physical plant has a team in the corner taking apart the air conditioning. You ordered chicken to go for twenty and the vice-president is a vegetarian. We've all experienced these hassles. They are the unglamorous details that now and then make or break a meeting, but almost always pop up in one form or another as troublesome distractions.

> Use a checklist for meeting preparation so none of the little details is overlooked. Better yet, train your assistant to handle this part of the planning so you can keep your mind on important items. Start by using or adapting the list given on page 71.

Step Five: Gauge Progress While You Are Running the Meeting

Don't be distracted by details nor swept up in the discussion at the expense of staying in charge. Are you sticking to the agenda? Are time limits respected? Are digressions pulled back? Are disputes getting out of hand? Is "Long-Winded Charlie" at it again?

CHECKLIST
FOR PLANNING MEETING DETAILS

Is the agenda firm? Distribute now or in meeting?

Do all participants know the meeting time and place?
- Is a map of the location necessary?
- Do they have required documents, papers, etc.?
- Are contributors clear on responsibilities?
- Do they know likely lunch or dinner plans?
- Is there a last-minute call-in number?
- Is a plan needed for substitute attendees?

Is the meeting room ready?
- Unlock early?
- Media equipment confirmed and checked?
- Enough seats?
- Plans made for room arrangement?
- Lighting OK?
- Phone or telecommunications services?
- Plans to stow equipment when completed?
- Do you need copier services?
- Heating, cooling OK?
- Sound equipment, acoustics?
- Rest room available?

Are plans made for recording minutes?

Does anything need a rehearsal?

Documents or reports for members to take from meeting?

Are you planning to evaluate the meeting?

Key telephone numbers for media services (   ); for physical plant (   ); for

leader's office (   ).

If digressions develop, actively remind the group that you wish to follow the agenda. If your strategy is a group-centered one, ask the group if they want to change the agenda (or have them review it at the outset). Postpone extra items or topics for later new business. Be strict. You are the only one there charged with keeping the meeting on track.

Watch your time. When possible, actively suggest time limits for certain parts of a discussion. Don't be hesitant to say "We have two more topics and fifteen minutes to go. How about no more than five minutes on the next item and ten on the last?" (Get the participants' agreement up front; it works.) Cut off Long-Winded Charlie directly ("How about only one more point, Charlie; we've got to move on.") Feel free to use a timer for presentations or discussion (the little five-minute egg timers are perfect and inexpensive). Calculate the per-minute cost of your meeting (salaries, overhead, lost work) and share it with the group.

Push for consensus when you can. Ask for action (suggest a motion to vote). Summarize pros and cons or ask protagonists to each give their wrap-up comments, then ask for a vote. Test for early readiness to vote; it will prompt the stakeholders into action. Don't be waylaid by trivial questions, but remember that they might be extremely important to the asker. (Say they will be handled later.) If you know that a participant is holding back, call on him or her. If the chronic complainer is about to go at it again, suggest that the comments come up later on the agenda. If you come to an absolute impasse, adjourn the meeting for thirty minutes for groups to ponder grounds for resolution.

Observe whether your group is working cohesively. Are they a team? Is there pride in being in the group? Do they have a positive identity? Do individuals seem to be gaining personal rewards from participation? Stress teamwork in your leader remarks. Praise the group as a whole. If you must reprimand, do it privately with individuals. Get the individuals to feel good as a group. Make participation rewarding.

Lead with purpose and participation foremost in mind.

Step Six: Take Care
of Necessary Follow-Ups
One of the weakest links between meetings and taking action is that once the decision has been made, not enough attention is given to responsibilities for implementation.

Double-check to insure that every decision for action also has a plan for implementation. Use the meeting to get agreements for the implementation plan. It is an effective basis for generating individual commitment.

Unless your meeting is a "one-shot" one, chances are that you have ongoing business. Use one meeting to plan the next.

Make the agenda for your next meeting the last item of business on your present one. Generate commitment for positive participation in the next meeting. Do anything possible to create a positive group spirit that will build from meeting to meeting. Are there any external rewards you can bestow? (Dinner? Cocktail hour? An especially pleasant meeting place? Coverage in the company newspaper?)

Have a system whereby individuals who missed the meeting will receive copies of reports as well as any minutes.

Having an active method for evaluating meetings from time to time yields two benefits. First, you'll see how participants are reacting to your leadership strategies. Second, they will develop more of a feeling of commitment if they are asked to do the evaluation.

Consider asking participants to evaluate their meeting. This can be done with simple paper-and-pencil questionnaires. Try the one below.

Permission to reproduce this form is given by the author and publisher. Frederick Williams, Executive Communication Power, Englewood Cliffs, N.J.: Prentice-Hall, Inc., 1982.

MEETINGS EVALUATION FORM

1. The meeting:

had clear goals___:___:___:___:___:___:___had unclear goals

met its goals___:___:___:___:___:___:___missed its goals

was efficient___:___:___:___:___:___:___was inefficient

2. The leader:

did a good job___:___:___:___:___:___:___did a poor job

encouraged participation___:___:___:___:___:___:___discouraged it

was dictatorial___:___:___:___:___:___:___was democratic

saved time___:___:___:___:___:___:___wasted time

3. As a participant, I:

fully contributed___:___:___:___:___:___:___did not contribute

spoke freely___:___:___:___:___:___:___spoke cautiously

felt rewarded___:___:___:___:___:___:___felt shortchanged

felt satisfied___:___:___:___:___:___:___felt dissatisfied

4. Comments:

13

Using
Telephone Strategies

The telephone is one of the most valuable executive communications tools. Just as you dress for success or double-check your correspondence for clarity and accuracy, you can do the same for your telephone strategies. What is your personal telephone image? Do your office staff members build or tarnish your executive style by their telephone manners?

WHAT THEY HEAR
IS WHAT THEY "SEE"

After about six months in the middle-executive ranks of a midwestern insurance firm, Richard K. accidentally caught a glimpse of the report from the head-hunting firm that had located him for the job. Because he had always thought his major managerial strengths were in his fiscal prowess, Richard was surprised to see the notation:

> . . . conveys a very alert and enthusiastic personality over the telephone. . . . very businesslike yet natural in his conversational manner. . . . obviously very bright and already experienced in executive style.

It seemed ironic that a Friday seminar on effective telephone sales strategies, taken almost eight years earlier when he was in marketing, had paid an extra dividend.

HOW'S YOUR IMAGE?

Your personal telephone image is a function of three main factors: your voice, your telephone manners, and the general image conveyed by anyone who answers the phone on behalf of you or your office.

Do You Sound as Good as You Could?

"Every time Mr. L. gets on the line, I think I'm getting a lewd telephone call," our receptionist regularly used to tell my secretary.

I couldn't feel sorry for Mr. L. because he was a Texas oil millionaire who could afford to sound any way he wanted. His problem was a bad habit of holding the mouthpiece so close that you could literally hear his lips smack between rasping breaths.

Obviously, most of us do not know how we sound over the phone, and there is no way to find out unless we make a special effort.

> Ask a few friends to tell you how you sound on the phone. Better yet, photocopy the form on page 76 and have your friends ask their secretaries or associates—preferably ones who do not know you—to fill in the scales when you make special calls to their offices. (Note below which of these scales refer to "voice.") Or, for another approach to the problem, record your voice on another line in your office or home. Fill in the scales yourself.

Four of the scales on page 76 refer directly to vocal characteristics. In brief, they are:

Clear: Do you speak distinctly rather than slurring words (especially endings)? Is your rate slow enough to be understood, but not so slow as to put the other person to sleep? Are you loud enough? Are your lips about an inch from the mouthpiece? Do you intentionally slow down and emphasize numbers or technical words (even spelling the latter)?

Expressive: Do the qualities of your voice convey the emotional meanings you wish to emphasize? Do you speak at a moderate rate? Do you vary your vocal pitch for emphasis? Do you avoid "breathiness"? Do you speak at a moderate volume? Do you sound awake, alert, and enthusiastic? Are you using effective vocal techniques of nonverbal communication (see Chapter 16)?

Pleasant: Do you avoid any mannerisms that convey unpleasantness— e.g., loud volume, a negative sounding "uh-huh" or "yeh," or failure to respond at all (which causes the speaker to wonder if you are listening)? Can you put a "smile" in your voice by conveying enthusiasm, interest, positive reactions, and a generally pleasing vocal quality?

Natural: Are you affecting a normal conversational style of language and vocal quality (remember Lily Tomlin's "One ringy-dingy" routine)? Are you avoiding technical terms and slang? As one secretary around our office puts it, "Is he for real?"

Permission to reproduce this form is given by the author and publisher. Frederick Williams, Executive Communication Power, *Englewood Cliffs, N.J.: Prentice-Hall, Inc., 1982.*

TELEPHONE PERSONALITY EVALUATION FORM

(Place one check mark per scale)

1. *The caller sounds:*

positive___:___:___:___:___:___:___negative
alert___:___:___:___:___:___:___lazy
happy___:___:___:___:___:___:___grumpy
educated___:___:___:___:___:___:___uneducated
careful___:___:___:___:___:___:___careless
courteous___:___:___:___:___:___:___rude
calm___:___:___:___:___:___:___emotional
trustworthy___:___:___:___:___:___:___untrustworthy

2. *The caller's speech and language are:*

clear___:___:___:___:___:___:___unclear
expressive___:___:___:___:___:___:___dull
natural___:___:___:___:___:___:___unnatural
pleasant___:___:___:___:___:___:___unpleasant

3. *How much would I like to conduct business with the caller?*

very much___:___:___:___:___:___:___not at all

What's Your Office Doing
for Your Image?

What's your favorite story? Calling the electric company about your bill? Calling the tax office? Mine is about calling the local office of the world's largest computer company. It took no less than ten tries (plus a few insults, infinite holds and "don't knows") to get an answer to a relatively simple technical question. But I must also admit that several of my own office tangles are too embarrassing to mention!

> Use the checklist on page 78 to evaluate the habits of those who represent you and your organization on the telephone. Trade evaluations with a friend in another office or organization.

You'll note that most of the items on the checklist are matters of courtesy and standard routine. None is difficult to institute. But take care to have procedures whereby break-time "fill-ins" or temporary workers learn the routines. A score total of twenty or over means you need work. Use the checklist as a part of your training program.

SEVEN TIPS FOR
WINNING WITH THE TELEPHONE

1. Periodically check your telephone style and image, including the image projected by your staff. (Use the rating form and checklist given earlier.) Don't have the most junior of your clerical staff serving as the telephone receptionist.

2. Have formal staff training (and updates) on telephone usage. (Again, use the rating and check-off sheets in this chapter as guides.) Your telephone company has free booklets and films for training purposes. They usually can also recommend a professional trainer if they do not do it themselves.

3. Know the advantages and disadvantages of the telephone as a communications medium. The telephone is personal, rapid, and inexpensive. It will get you immediate feedback from the other person. But it is an oral mode, so complex descriptions are more difficult than if they are done in writing or with the use of drawings. Perhaps you do not need or want immediate feedback. Also, there is always the chance that you are calling the other party at the wrong time—e.g., the person could be angry about

Permission to reproduce this form is given by the author and publisher. Frederick Williams, Executive Communication Power, *Englewood Cliffs, N.J.: Prentice-Hall, Inc., 1982.*

CHECKLIST FOR OFFICE TELEPHONE PROCEDURES

1 = yes, always   2 = yes and no   3 = seldom

1. (   ) Does the office answer the phone at least by the third ring?

2. (   ) Can staff members transfer calls to the proper party in one step?

3. (   ) Can they usually avoid putting callers on hold longer than fifteen seconds except for infrequent and unavoidable reasons?

4. (   ) When an individual called is not available, are standard and appropriate phrases used? (Don't say, "He's out for coffee," but "He's away from his desk." Be sure to include (a) "May I or anyone else help you?" and (b) "May I have him return your call?")

5. (   ) Can callers depend upon accurate messages being taken by receptionists? (Spell unusual names because it is very embarrassing for a follow-up caller to ask for a wrong name. Jot down notes if the pronunciation is unusual. Read back telephone numbers to double-check them. Don't forget to get area codes. Be sure the message reaches the called party.)

6. (   ) Is your staff effective in placing calls? (What image do they project to the called parties? Do they have full information for calling? Do they know how to get special numbers? Do they know rate differences for calling? Do they wait for eight to ten rings before hanging up?)

7. (   ) Do you have an office policy for screening calls according to the priorities set by the persons called? (Is proper phrasing used for screening? If there is a possibility of the call not being taken at the moment, it may be necessary to say that the called person is "not available at the moment." It's advisable to add, "May I tell Mrs. Thornton the nature of your call?" Obviously, this must be done tactfully and with agreed-upon procedures. Do all persons, including temporaries, know the procedures?)

8. (   ) Do your staff members know the names of VIP callers and have procedures for treating them accordingly?

9. (   ) Do you have procedures whereby the staff will know the whereabouts of individuals likely to receive important calls but who are not in their offices? (Are phone itineraries prepared for traveling executives and priorities set for VIP callers?)

10. (   ) Do you have a regular training program for staff members who answer your phone frequently? Are performances periodically checked?

something, tired, or preoccupied. Finally, most executives want important messages in writing before they can be formalized.

4. If you screen calls, be certain that it is done properly. The main problem is that you can easily create the image that you feel callers are unimportant. Agree on priorities with your secretary or receptionist; for example:

> Urgent—Get the call through to you wherever you are.
>
> Important—Put the call through if you are available. If you are not, then be certain the message is delivered to you promptly.
>
> Routine—Only put the call through if you are easily free to take it. Otherwise take the message and have it available for you with other routine items.
>
> Option or Screen Out—Don't bother you with taking the call. Take a brief message with the caller's reason for telephoning. Promise only to bring it to the called person's attention. Try to handle the answer to the caller, making no callback necessary.

5. Use notes; take notes. If you handle many clients or accounts, keep a summary note file so you can let the other party know that you remember their needs—e.g., "Yes, how did the new bearings we sent last year work out?" Have a special colored telephone note pad so you know anything written on this paper was from a telephone call. When you are about to make an important call, write out the points you want to be sure to make.

6. Watch your time. Limit the length of your conversations to getting the job done. Know when to hang up. If you have more than one or two important calls to make during the day, set aside a time, have all of your numbers and notes ready, get comfortable, then make them all. If you only wish to leave a message for the other party, call when that person is not likely to be in. If you want to get directly to a party and not be put off, call when the person is likely to be in. Try calling early, during their secretary's lunch break, or late, when they have no one to screen their calls. Remember that people are likely to be fresher and more positive early in the day. Don't forget time-zone differences.

7. Put telephone technologies to work for you. If you are on the phone for long periods or need both hands free, consider a small earphone set. Look out for "squawk boxes" (speaker phones), because you never know who might be listening. If you make many calls from a list of twenty to thirty

numbers, consider getting a rapid-dial unit. If you need to be directly available to certain individuals, have a private line installed and share the number accordingly. Consider the advantage of telephone conferencing— i.e., with more than one other person on the line.

14

Handling Office Sex Talk

One of the most visible consequences of the women's revolution has been the move into professional and managerial ranks of the modern female executive. It has been a sure victory for women's rights. Moreover, most men will agree that the formerly male management environment is all the more productive and interesting because of the change. At the same time, however, both male and female executives have their challenges cut out for them: How do you draw the line between the excitement of male-female teamwork and the potential for deeper sexual involvement? Further, the specter of sexual harassment has been made more visible by gains in employment rights. We all enjoy talk with the opposite sex, but how does a professional relationship deal with sexual attraction? How does idle sex talk become harassment?

HOW DO YOU DO BUSINESS WITH SOMEONE WHO INTERESTS YOU SEXUALLY?

One of the most visible changes of the last decade is that the office is no longer the bastion of male management. Men and women are having to learn rapidly how to relate as professional colleagues, and this has brought its share of strain. Men have had to learn that there can be more topics for office small talk than women, sports, and shady jokes. Women are under personal pressure to prove their professionalism without desexing themselves. How can men and women work successfully together without getting into eventually negative sexual entanglements, yet preserve those qualities which make for pleasant everyday human relationships?

The following responses were culled from interviews, seminar discussions, and a few reports found in public media.

Women's Notes

Gloria is around thirty-five, has been married for twelve years, says she's happy, and is working her way up in marketing in the telephone company.

> I've had more problems being accepted as a serious professional since I moved into management five years ago than I've had with any of the sexual problems of working with men. I know that I'm attractive enough to get their attention, but this business has had such a long history of only having women as secretaries or switchboard operators that there is a longtime tradition around here for men not to be involved with female employees. If you needed to have lunch or dinner with a man around here, it would either have to be on the sly or with a group. If I ever said anything sexually provocative in the office, I'd be in trouble fast. This place has still not changed so I can be comfortable as a woman manager. If my career weren't going so well and my marriage OK, I'd get out.

Helen is twenty-eight, single, recently divorced, and a management trainee with a department store chain:

> I haven't had any trouble mixing a possible relationship with getting along in my job. Clark is another trainee I met here a few months back, and we're dating pretty regularly now. How can that be wrong? I do my work and he does his. We're grownups—we don't hold hands on the job. But he does kiss me and talk sweet when we go out to lunch together, which is about twice a week. If the company didn't like us dating or even getting married, I'd tell them to shove it. After all, I spend most of my waking hours around this place. How else will I ever meet somebody?

Sheila is a professional administrator in the health-care area. She is forty, has never married, and has an on-again, off-again relationship with Ken, a resident physician.

> It's tough to mix career with a relationship. I feel very close to Ken and for a while we lived together. He's talked about marriage, but I know that one of us would have to leave our job here. And I've given my all to building my career, including never marrying. You know, I got into management before the "women's thing" broke. [Sheila had taken care of an invalid mother who recently passed away.] But I've got to be frank about it. Every time I handle some paperwork here for Ken, I can't separate my feelings from my work. Sometimes I now think that we are either going to have to get married or call it quits for good. There's just too much stress with things as they are.

Mary is twenty-six and a buyer for a discount store. She does well in her work, but also has a reputation for dressing and speaking provocatively.

> Sure I like men—what woman doesn't? And I get my kicks from kidding around with them. Why not hug a guy who goes home every night to three screaming kids and a wife who hasn't taken her bathrobe off all day? Men like a pretty face and they will do things for you. Really, I think I can do better with

82

some of our suppliers than most of our male buyers. And I don't buy the lunches either! Just one rule, though—I don't go to bed with any of them. Not around here, at least. It would get too complicated.

Male Reflections

Larry is forty-two, married, with four children, and gets along very well with his male—but not female—management colleagues in an insurance firm.

> I don't think I have anything against women in management, but I can't relate to most of them. If you say anything about them as "women," they call you a "sexist bigot." I wouldn't even give one flowers for fear of being reported to the government. Mess around? Not with any of these types! The ones on their way up have forgotten they're women. And the rest won't last!

Herb is single, dates in and out of the company, and is in his midtwenties.

> Women in management are OK, but there are two big problems. First, have you ever noticed that women don't tend to get along with each other? Just be sure you don't get between a couple of them when they're on the warpath. Second, you have to be careful how you talk to them. They're good workers and managers, but so many are self-conscious about being women. Still, I sure like having them around.

Brian has just been married for the second time. He is forty-four, works on the staff of a university, and was particularly hesitant to tell his story.

> I was absolutely stunned the first time I saw Jean—she's manager of student financial aid. Seeing a good-looking woman in charge of twenty-five employees really impressed me. I must have fantasized about her for a month before I asked her out for a drink. And we really hit it off. But guess what? It was the reverse of the old story. She was the one who was married. We had a two-month-long affair until it got to be too much for the both of us—ducking friends, her making excuses for being out late, and the silly stuff of giving each other secret notes on campus. I think the strain got to her. She went on a few months' unpaid leave and told me she didn't want to see me until she felt better about things. The next thing I heard was that she had taken another job. Then just last week a mutual friend told me she'd gotten divorced. Funny thing—I had gotten remarried that same week.

Peter works in a big city ad agency. He is in his early thirties, has never married, and is financially successful.

> There are no rules in the advertising world if you're good at what you do— that is, if you make big money. I can take any girl out here, including some of the lady account executives, and the company doesn't give a damn about it if business is good. There is plenty of office hanky-panky, too—including some long boy-girl lunch breaks. Just one thing to remember: Even when you go to bed, don't get involved.

No Easy Answers

There are no quick and ready solutions to the problem of doing business with someone who interests you sexually. How you communicate will vary with a number of factors, including the kind of office or organization and your own value system.

What's the atmosphere around your office? How do men and women communicate to each other? If you want to stay and feel comfortable, you'll have to adjust to it.

Can you feel natural and productive in this environment? Can you communicate without being self-conscious about it? If you're a woman and you have to go to extremes to talk like "one of the guys," you might think of other alternatives, including getting out.

Don't assume that everybody, especially the opposite sex, sees the office atmosphere in the same way you do. Watch how others communicate. Shape your own communications appropriately from person to person.

Look out for company rules about office relationships or behavior. Probably nobody will fire you these days for falling in love, but these kinds of rules can be used against you for other reasons.

Is your relationship comfortable enough for you to feel that now (or soon) you would not be embarrassed to have anybody—friends, boss, co-workers—know about it? Will you be able to communicate openly to the other person as well as to outsiders? If not, you'll possibly be limiting your communication effectiveness in other areas, plus carrying added stress on the job. You'll have to decide if it is worth the added strain.

In the minds of both of you, is the relationship important enough that one of you will change jobs if necessary? Can you openly discuss it? Can you negotiate such agreements? (If you cannot, then one of you, or both, is going to lose—professionally or personally.)

When challenged because of your sex role, can you handle it personally? Can you set the line clearly in a relationship?

If you are a man who is being chided or berated by a woman about sex-role stereotyping, can you discuss the matter rationally, trying to see the basis for the misunderstanding? Can you attack the problem and not the person (see Chapter 3)? Can you find common ground as professionals (see Chapter 5)? Can you take losing the skirmish if you may eventually come out ahead in the war (a trusting and productive professional relationship)?

If you are a woman, can you handle comments like "Poor little thing," "Are you available?" or "Sleeping your way up?" Better yet, can you privately discuss your problem in a positive and constructive manner? ("It makes it hard to relate to you as a professional when you say . . .") Sexual harassment is discussed in the next section.

Can you say no when you mean it and it is important to do so? For men, if a woman who is attracted to you asks you for a drink or suggests lunch alone with you, can you decline (if you feel the need to) in a way not embarrassing to either of you? For women, can you turn down a man's invitation for lunch or drinks without turning off a friendship or a productive professional relation-ship? Can you draw the final line between enjoying one another and getting into a dead-end affair? Or, for both men and women, if you want to play it out, can you be honest enough with each other to discuss where you think it is all going?

The modern office offers us great potential to work together productively as men and women. You will benefit from this progress if you can be clear about the relation between your personal attraction to the opposite sex and your goals as a true professional. It's possible, but it takes thought and effective communication.

COURTING DISASTER

Even as talk with members of the opposite sex can be a source of genuine pleasure, abuses and misunderstandings can lead to professional disaster.

Tony's Story

Tony, twenty-eight and single, was working hard to get onto the central manage-ment staff of a grocery chain. He also enjoyed his reputation as the staff "stud" in the company's flagship market, where he was assistant manager. Part of his reputation came from his constant kidding around with the female checkers—calling them sweet names, squeezing a shoulder now and then, and bringing them treats. In this respect, Tony was not only harmless, but he made the checkers feel better in their usually dreary days. But most of his reputation was built on rumors and inferences about his sexual prowess which he actively nourished around his male colleagues.

This reputation came to figure in Tony's future with the company when he was genuinely attracted to Marina, a new member of the accounting staff. She was a young woman of Latin American origin whom Tony felt was showing interest in him when she would respond with a fluttering smile to his informal banter. She also seemed to dress more provocatively than her peers, which was also especially exciting to Tony.

All this led Tony to staying around late, pretending to help with the store's closing, but really paying increasing attention to Marina, and finally to the point of asking her out for a drink. To Tony's amazement, Marina recoiled in shock to the invitation and began to gather up her personal belongings as if to get away from him. Without thinking, he instinctively grabbed her by the arms, meaning to say that he was really serious about dating. In a panic response, Marina pressed the security alarm. Within a minute, Tony was faced with one security guard, an off-duty police officer, a sobbing Marina (who thought she was about to be attacked), and five minutes later by the store's senior manager.

Tony never worked another day for the grocery chain; Marina was given two weeks' vacation and a transfer to another store for not pressing charges which the off-duty officer offered to initiate.

Although Tony's story—especially its sorry ending—is not an everyday event, almost anyone who has worked in an organization where the sexes are mixed has experienced parts of it. This is especially true where status differences invite sexual harassment.

Tony hadn't counted on two critical factors which set the stage for his downfall. First, although his reputation as the store Romeo was considered as mostly harmless banter by the men, some of the women took it seriously enough to warn new female employees about him. Marina was one of them. Second, Marina came from a background where although the women may seem to dress provocatively to "outsiders," the male and female courtship routines are very formal. A serious suitor does not talk sexually—even light banter—in public to the woman. (Tony had misread Marina's "fluttering" smile. It was actually one of anxiety.) Nor, without going through the family, do you ask for a date. (Asking directly is to assume that the woman has neither family nor reputation.)

Tony was not only a victim of how banter can turn to serious rumor across sex lines, but of his inability to read cultural differences in male-female relationships.

Handling Sexual Harassment

Fortunately, women are no longer powerless when faced with undesired advances or outright dicta ("Let's spend the weekend somewhere comfortable and have a long-range discussion about your career"). Sex discrimination has been defined under federal law as violation of fair employment practices.

Cases of sexual harassment have become sufficiently visible in instances of prosecution that many organizations have actively pursued formal preventative measures.

> Check to see if your organization has a formal policy about sexual harassment—one that includes concrete definitions of what constitutes violations and details the procedures for reporting it (procedures that hopefully are not traumatic for the victim).
>
> Has this policy been sufficiently administered to ferret out serious offenders? If it has not, then there are grounds for complaint to federal and possibly state authorities.
>
> Has your organization set up informational or training sessions on the problems of sexual harassment, as well as the nature of their formal policy for combating it?

In the absence of a company policy, what can you do as an individual victim? Experts agree that everybody is better off if parties to the problem can try to handle it first, before taking formal action.

Talk to the offender outright about it if you feel confident (and safe) enough to do it. The verbal response may be negative or mixed, but the harassment may stop. Appeal on grounds of professionalism.

If talking doesn't halt the problem, write a personal letter stating what you consider to be wrong. Be specific. Consider sending it by registered mail so you have evidence of its delivery.

Keep a record—dates, times, places, what happened—of the harassments. This may be useful for your letter. And it may be necessary as part of a formal complaint if you must go that far.

THE BRIGHT SIDE

Despite the lingering specter of sexual harassment and the everyday challenges of men and women working as professional equals, it's becoming increasingly easy to see the bright side in this type of change. After all, we have added another 50 percent of our population to the outstanding executive talent pool. Opportunities for women have never been better.

And most of us feel that professional life is a lot more rewarding, if not outright fun.

IV

SELF TUNE-UPS

There are simple tactics that will help you to brush up your speaking, listening, reading, writing, body language, and even memory skills. They will not change you drastically overnight, but you'll be able to feel the benefits as you put them to work to increase your communication power.

15

Your Speech: Stand Up, Speak Up, Shut Up

There is hardly a communication skill that benefits the modern executive more than being able to speak on his or her feet. Unlike yesteryear, the modern speechmaker seeks not so much to present an image of silver-tongued oratory, but to gain influence and understanding. You can accomplish this by employing the principles of motivation (see Chapters 2–6) along with the keys to effective speech planning and delivery. With preparation, practice, and persistence, you can do much to further your career through effective public speaking.

IS SPEAKING A CHALLENGE OR AN OPPORTUNITY FOR YOU?

What About a "Gift of Gab"?

Each of us has at some time been presented with the opportunity to speak before a group. It may be a brief report at a Rotary Club, a sales presentation to a group of buyers, a talk at the local PTA, or a summary of a new benefits package for our employees. We typically respond to such opportunities in one of three ways:

- About 20 percent of us come up with sufficiently complex excuses to avoid public speaking altogether. The thought of getting up in front of other people terrifies us. We become highly skilled at avoiding it entirely.

- About 60 percent of us struggle through the experience—shakes, dry mouth, and all. We are somewhat less effective than we would like to be, but we have met the challenge, as uncomfortable as it is.

- About 20 percent of us actively look forward to speaking to others. We are sometimes a bit nervous too, but we are able to channel much of this nervousness into the excitement of our presentation. We expect to be effective and we usually are. Our speech experience is enjoyable. We know that the more we speak to groups, the more effective we will become.

Any of us can be in the 20 percent who welcome the chance to speak. You can make public speaking a winning opportunity for yourself. Does this come naturally—the so-called gift of gab?

No, not at all. There is no gift of gab. Making speeches is like any other learned human behavior, from cooking to swinging a golf club. You are not born with it. You must learn the basics. You must practice and then improve with experience. Because of such factors as personality, experiences with groups as a child, and the opportunity to learn the principles of speech making, some people have an easier time than others in improving their performance before groups. But almost anyone who has the will to persist can improve through knowledge and practice.

Success Stories

Improved speech is a direct method for becoming a more effective person. For example:

Hilda R. was a secretary for a local telephone company who signed up for a volunteer speaker group because her social life was so dull. Although she had never considered herself to be a public speaker, Hilda traded the challenge of ten hours of professional speech training for the prospects of getting around to meet new and different people. A few years later, when the company modernized and moved women into more than secretarial and switchboard jobs, Hilda was one of the first to move directly into the marketing department. She now teaches an in-company speech class in her spare time.

Will F. took an evening university class in speaking so he could feel less uneasy in his sales presentations. Not only did his professional career advance, but he found himself becoming increasingly influential in civic affairs as he was called upon to chair new committees and to make public presentations. He ran for local office and was elected. Even in his most optimistic view, Will never thought he would come to enjoy getting up in front of people.

Then there is Bob A., a senior vice-president of a rapidly growing computer-services corporation. As talented as Bob is, he may never be president of his company or any other. He is so dull when he gets up in front of a group that he has become a company joke. Bill knows this, so he always begins his presentation by apologizing for being so dull. The trouble is that people believe him!

USE THE THREE KEYS
TO EFFECTIVE SPEAKING

Most of us can master these three simple keys for success in public speaking. They are not difficult to understand. But they take practice and persistence to accomplish. You must learn to do the following:

1. Target your audience and purpose.
2. Organize for results.
3. Develop your delivery.

Even if you are a skilled speaker, try these. They will make you even better.

FIRST KEY:
TARGET YOUR AUDIENCE
AND PURPOSE

Speak With Purpose

We might title this section "How to Take Aim at Your Audience," because your only legitimate reason for speaking to a group is to get them to react in a specific way. Usually we have one of three dominant purposes:

- to get our audience to understand something
- to get them to believe or act in a certain way
- to have them feel interested or entertained

We say "dominant" because almost any speech has a mixture of information, persuasion, and interest or entertainment. Almost any presentation you will ever give to a group—from a sales briefing to a eulogy—will reflect the above purposes.

> For your speech, jot down the statement of your specific purpose. This statement should incorporate (1) the dominant purpose (to inform, persuade, or entertain), (2) identification of your audience, and (3) reference to your subject matter.

Be result-oriented in stating your specific purpose. Imagine that you are a bystander meeting people coming from your presentation and have the chance to ask them what you said. What one thing would you most want them to remember?

Here are some sample purpose statements:

- "To get our marketing group to understand the reason for our recent price changes."
- "To persuade the sales staff to make better use of the new prospect sheets we've given them."
- "To get the clients loosened up, relaxed, for the afternoon meeting; to entertain them briefly during lunch."

The dominant speech purposes need no further explanation except to say that *entertainment* does not necessarily mean rolling them in the aisles. It refers more to the basic notion of any kind of communication that is itself pleasurable or immediately rewarding. You feel good hearing it. It can be speech material that has high human-interest value—personal anecdotes, examples, things of beauty.

Most speeches have secondary purposes. Obviously, when we are giving a speech to gain understanding, we are also doing some persuading. Or in order to keep our audience interested in a topic, we may entertain them a little.

> Add to your overall purpose statement any special considerations you have about secondary purposes. This may be an audience that you will have to entertain a little in order to get them interested in your persuasion. Or you may have to persuade them that it is important for them to understand your point.

Write out your total purpose or target statement on a single sheet or card and keep it in front of you during the entire planning of your speech. Make it the first entry in your speech notes.

Know Your Audience

Planning a speech has much in common with market research. You have a "product" (your message) which you want the audience to "buy" (accept). The more your message can be delivered in a form tailored to the interests and needs of your audience, the better are your chances of success. To meet the audience needs, you will want to know three main types of information:

- their knowledge of and interest in your topic
- their attitudes about you
- their expectations of the speech occasion

> Find out the level of audience knowledge in your topic as a baseline upon which to build your speech content. Audiences are never so bored as when you are telling them what they already know. Audience attitudes toward your subject will be the basis for gauging how many interest-raising devices you will want to use.

The "need to know" and "want to believe" rules are handy interpretations of audience analysis. The less an audience is already interested in a topic, the more you will have to persuade or entertain them in order to gain their understanding. The less they want to believe something, the more you may need to use information and entertainment along with your primary purpose of persuasion.

> Find out audience attitudes about you as a basis for determining the amount and type of content you will need to build your credibility with them.

If possible, convey information about yourself in any mailing or packets distributed prior to your presentation. Be doubly certain that whoever introduces you says what you most need to have said. Your personal image is a major factor in getting people to understand or believe you. Audience analysis will help you decide how much common ground you will have to build. It will also suggest materials for your speech introduction and conclusion.

> Always double-check on the nature of the speech occasion. Know what the audience expects. Be sure that your speech purpose and subsequent materials are consonant with these expectations.

Some speech occasions—e.g., civic clubs, stockholders' meetings, testimonial dinners, professional associations, even sales presentations—may be more ritualized than you expect. You can often benefit by finding out about other speakers and speeches. Even when you go to different parts of your own organization, especially if it is a large one, you may find rather rigid rules about length of presentation, humor, taking questions, length and type of discussion, and the like. Nothing falls flatter than a five-minute comedy bit when the audience expects a few words of inspiration. Know also what may be happening before and after your speech. You may have to make some adjustments if your audience is drifting in from a heavy lunch (or if people are on the edge of their chairs at 4:45 P.M.).

SECOND KEY: ORGANIZE FOR RESULTS

The biggest mistake you can make in getting ready to assemble your speech is to assume that you can effectively write it out from beginning to end. (How many times have you heard, "I spent all day trying to write my speech"?) Quite the contrary, as any experienced speaker will tell you, 90 percent of speech preparation is in the planning, not the writing. In fact, you may never write anything other than your research notes and an outline.

Plan Your Main Ideas

The most efficient strategy to begin organizing your speech is to plan ideas, not words.

Every bit of content in your speech should be aimed at achieving results. Don't waste your time or your audience's.

Think of your speech purpose first in planning the materials for your presentation. Given what you know about your audience, what will it take to achieve your speech purpose? Jot down the major points you will want to get across. (Use three-by-five-inch cards or scratch paper that you will be able to move around.)

Double-check that the points support your main purpose. Don't worry yet about the order for delivering them.

Plan the body of your speech first, not the introduction. Organize from the top (most important ideas) down (the details). Do this by laying out your note cards on a large table or on a bulletin board (use colored pushpins to identify clusters of related items). Rearrange these materials until you have the structure that best supports your speech purpose. Make notes on details at this point and fit them into your arrangement.

Organize the Delivery Sequence

Usually the most formal and logical structure of your materials is not in precisely the same form as you will deliver it to your audience. You must translate a hierarchy into a sequence.

Return to your notes with the goal of putting them into the most persuasive, most understandable, and most interesting format for your audience. Rearrange your note cards for a delivery sequence. Position your audience in your mind's eye, then talk through your newly arranged notes as if your presentation were simply a form of enlarged conversation.

Keep talking through your notes until you are comfortable with the sequence. Then jot down this best delivery sequence as your notes for your eventual speech.

Plan the Introduction and Conclusion

Think of the body of your speech as a package of ideas about to be delivered. It will need a few words of introduction and a few of conclusion. These words should be closely tied to the interests and attitudes of your audience. They are like greetings and farewells. They should be personal.

Plan an introduction that will (1) get attention, (2) create a good feeling about you, and (3) lead into your topic. Make it personal. Keep it brief.

Jokes are effective attention getters, but unless your joke is especially appropriate to the occasion, use something else. Don't resort to the stereotype of "something funny happened to me on the way here."

You can also start by asking your audience a question. Or you can compliment them. Relate a brief anecdote (it must have high interest value) which stresses the importance of your topic. Present some striking or unusual statistics. Use common ground (motives you and your audience share; see Chapter 5) strategies for linking yourself with your audience. Be sure that your credentials are out front. Be friendly. The most effective method for leading into your speech is to preview it. But be sure to do it briefly.

Finally, remember: Do not apologize (too many inexperienced speakers reveal themselves by doing this, and it's also a bore).

> Plan a conclusion that (1) stresses the dominant purpose of your speech, (2) leaves a positive impression of you, and (3) has a clear climax or ending note.

Summaries are almost always the most effective strategy for reinforcing your main points with your audience. If you can, tie the summary in with their personal motives ("the three things most important for *you* . . ."). Sometimes a clever key word or visualization will greatly facilitate the audience's ability to remember your point (remember Churchill's *V* for victory?). *I* and *we* words will lend your personal touch and increase your apparent sincerity. Be sure to have a conclusion that says *end*. It is a disaster for you as well as your audience if they have to guess whether you have concluded or not. (One way to salvage the situation is for you or the moderator to break in, saying, "We may have time for a few questions.") Take care, too, that dramatic materials used too soon in your conclusion do not cause premature applause. Save them for the end.

Review Your Overall Plan

It is often helpful if you can get away from the planning process at this point for a few hours or even a few days. Time will give you the benefit of a fresh perspective when you come back to look over your ideas. You'll find, too, that once you get a speech going in your mind, you will keep on preparing it subconsciously. You'll be able to use those spare moments while commuting, or waiting at the bank, to mull the ideas over and over again in your mind. Your speech content will improve with age.

Finally, the simplest and most effective advice for speech organization is:

- Tell them what you're going to say.
- Say it.
- Tell them what you've said.

THIRD KEY:
DEVELOP YOUR DELIVERY

Many a presentation stands or falls—no matter the quality of its content—on how the speaker looks (visual), sounds (vocal), and uses language (verbal). Working the three V's can make or break your success in front of groups. Delivery effectiveness is critically important when your audience may not be interested in you or your topic, when your credibility is vague or doubted by your audience, or when your audience is outright hostile toward you or your ideas. It is correspondingly less critical when there is a strong "need to know" or "want to believe" attitude on the part of your audience. (This is why ministers with captive congregations or engineers giving technical reports can get by although they are dull.) Yet you will almost always observe that the most successful leaders, executives, and managers have the capability to appear interested, authoritative, and clear in their spoken communications.

If you are worried about nervousness in getting up in front of others, consult the practical advice given in Chapter 8. Don't worry, you can handle the problem. Plenty of other people have.

The Verbal: How You Say It

The essence of your presentation is, of course, the words you use to convey your thoughts, opinions, admonitions, visualizations, arguments, and most fundamentally, your main points. Should you write these out carefully prior to giving your presentation? Probably not. Your speech will then sound written and it will be dull.

> You will usually be the most effective when you speak extemporaneously from notes. The notes will keep you organized and will prompt your memory. Yet your language will be natural and fluent. You will be perceived as more knowledgeable and more sincere if you seem to know what you are saying instead of having to read word for word from a manuscript.
>
> Notes are fair game. In fact, if you do not have notes and are highly fluent, you may be perceived as being too smooth (as if you've delivered your pitch a thousand times). Or if you are not fluent, people will think that you haven't prepared.

Memorized speeches are a thing of the past. The effort is not worth it. If it is important to you, it is possible to memorize your main points so you need not rely on written notes.

Although there may be occasions when reading from manuscript is necessary (as in delivering a formal statement to the press) for accuracy, you should avoid it. You will lose most of the advantages of the oral situation—spontaneity, interaction, and effective visual gestures (especially eye contact).

Again, plan the language of your presentation by talking through your speech notes. Position your audience and speak in a conversational manner. As "enlarged conversation," your language will be slightly more formal and your points better organized than in typical conversation. Practice this until your words flow easily. Perhaps you will want to include a few important words in your notes so that you will be sure to use them. Include your introduction and conclusion in these sessions.

As you become fluent in delivering your ideas, look for ways to improve. Start polishing.

As you compose and practice the language of your presentation, use the following checklist of questions:

1. Am I using words that are direct, concise, and especially meaningful for my audience (not overly technical, too simple, etc.)?
2. Am I avoiding "loaded" (overly emotional or argumentative) language?
3. Am I avoiding mushy or noncommittal words ("maybe," "probably," "I think")?
4. Am I speaking in the active voice ("John took it") rather than the passive ("It was taken by John")?
5. Am I using the present verb tense?
6. Do I use transition devices between major sections ("Therefore . . . ," "The third point . . . ," "Next . . .")?
7. Am I using language that has me talking *with* rather than *at* my audience?

Seriously consider making a tape recording of your practice run-through. Evaluate it yourself and, if possible, get another person to hear it. Have them rate it in terms of the evaluation scales given at the conclusion of this chapter.

The Vocal: How You Sound

Think for a moment how many ways you can say: "This has been a critical year for the company." Without changing a word of this sentence, you can sound as if you are talking about a pending receivership or you can convey the feeling that this has been the best sales year in history. You could also convey the message that you were angry, sad, nervous, distracted, happy, in a rush, unconcerned, or even plain confused. You could also sound very old or very young, masculine or feminine, or in excellent or poor health. The point is that how we say our words often conveys as much meaning as what we say.

Analyze your personal vocal qualities from a tape recording or from the comments of a thoughtful listener. Are there any qualities that are conveying a wrong message? Change them. As you polish your speech, try reinforcing your verbal meaning with vocal ones. Check on these items:

1. Can I be heard?
2. Do I sound odd in any way that I can correct?
3. Do I sound interested and enthusiastic?
4. Do my variations in pitch and loudness complement my speech purpose?
5. Do I sound fluent and confident?

The most effective voice qualities are those that totally reinforce what you are saying verbally and at the same time have a pleasing variation in pitch, rate, and volume. You do not have to sound overly feminine, masculine, old, or weak. If you think you have problems that are beyond your control, consult with a professional—a local teacher of public speaking, a speech and hearing clinician, or a voice coach. It could change your image for the better.

Should you use a microphone?

Take absolutely no chances that you will be poorly heard (especially in hotel meeting rooms with overall poor acoustics as well as noise coming through thin room dividers). Be sure you know how your voice sounds over a mike. Realize, too, that if you are free from a microphone, you have much more opportunity for gestures.

The Visual: How You Look

Body language has received much attention in the last several decades. Like your voice, your body also communicates messages to your audience—your confidence, sincerity, enthusiasm, anxiety, and even your attitudes toward your listeners.

Analyze your body language. Have a thoughtful critic analyze how you look. Use the checklist below (or see Chapter 16 for more details). Best yet, have a videotape made. Does your body convey the general positive messages that you wish? Answer these questions:

1. Do I look directly at my audience, thus conveying sincerity?
2. Is my posture erect, conveying health and alertness?
3. Do I look generally pleasant? Do I smile from time to time?
4. Am I avoiding actions that are annoying to my audience (rocking on my feet, glancing out of the window)?
5. Am I using common and direct gestures to reinforce points that I am making verbally?
6. Am I channeling nervous bodily movements (hand or knee shaking, face twitching) into more normal and positive bodily movements?
7. Does the sum of my gestures have me talking *with* rather than *at* my audience?

What about visual aids—flip chart, overhead slides, chalkboard, or models? Sure, use them, but be sure that they support your speech purpose.

> Consider how visual aids can improve your presentation. But don't get so involved with them that they become more important than your speech itself. Stay in personal command. Don't fade into the darkness as you turn the audience's attention over to your slides. Be sure your aids are supporting you—not vice versa!

Overuse of visual aids distracts from your personal communications potential. Also, you probably already know that whatever can go wrong with equipment is bound to happen to you, so be ready for problems. (Always test your own equipment well enough ahead to fix it if necessary. Never trust hotel or commercial operators.) If you do wish to use projection equipment, use overhead or rear projection so you can keep the house lights up. Otherwise you may put your audience to sleep.

INTERACTION IS THE NAME OF THE GAME

Times have changed. For centuries, impressiveness and control over others was stressed in the training of speakers. The modern audience is too sophisticated to tolerate this attitude for long in any speaker.

Again, talk *with* rather than *at* your audience. This involves all three of the keys to success in making speeches and presentations. You will want to share your excitement with your audience rather than keeping it one-sided. When you plan your speech with results foremost in mind, you will be one step ahead toward achieving your results. After all, the audience is ultimately more interested in the consequences of your speech upon themselves than they are in how you perform as a speaker. Common ground is a powerful device for modern persuasion.

The three V's of delivery serve to position you in the minds of your audience. Your language choice can be clear and appealing to your audience, or it can set you apart. *We* and *us* words will get you together with your audience. Your voice can be pleasing and reinforcing, or it can totally distract from your presentation. Your visual image will be carefully read by most audience members because they will believe what it is saying before they believe the words you are using.

Interaction in modern speaking also stresses invitations for questions and discussion. Leave time for them and prepare yourself to answer anything. An attention-getting question will set you up to give an equally attention-getting response.

Finally, remember that brevity pays. When the world news can be broadcast in fifteen minutes, few people have the patience to listen to you talk about anything for a much longer period. So again: Stand up, speak up, then shut up!

Permission to reproduce the form on page 103 is given by the author and publisher. Frederick Williams, Executive Communication Power, *Englewood Cliffs, N.J.: Prentice-Hall, Inc., 1982.*

SPEAKER EVALUATION FORM

The speaker's main point or points were:

1.

2.

3.

4.

The speech content was:
(place one check mark on each scale)

Clear____:____:____:____:____:____:____Unclear
Interesting____:____:____:____:____:____:____Dull
Well Organized____:____:____:____:____:____:____Disorganized
Convincing to me____:____:____:____:____:____:____Unconvincing
Relevant to me____:____:____:____:____:____:____Irrelevant
Accurate____:____:____:____:____:____:____Inaccurate
Factual____:____:____:____:____:____:____Distorted

The speaker seemed:

At ease____:____:____:____:____:____:____Ill at ease
Enthusiastic____:____:____:____:____:____:____Bored
Sincere____:____:____:____:____:____:____Insincere
Well prepared____:____:____:____:____:____:____Ill prepared
To talk at me____:____:____:____:____:____:____To talk with me
Confident____:____:____:____:____:____:____Unsure

Relative to other speakers I've heard,
I'd rate this one as:

The best____:____:____:____:____:____:____the worst

Other comments:

16

Your Body:
Is It Saying
Something Different?

People will believe what your body says even if you're trying to use words to say something different. You'll make the situation even worse if you try to hide your body language. What does your body say when you are trying to manage people? How well can you "read" the body language of your boss? What is the body language of successful executives and how can you learn it?

THE FIRST TWO MINUTES

Wally F. is a professional recruiter. Each spring he visits dozens of college campuses to interview aspiring young executives for a major oil company. On most other business days of the year, Wally meets up to six people a day who are looking for a management position with his company. Wally likes his work, but most of all he loves the seminar he teaches each fall in a local university on the art of interviewing.

Along with assigning over one hundred pages of reading on the nitty-gritty of job applications and screening on opening night, Wally requires his students to play a little poker each week.

"You see," explains Wally, "you've got to learn to read people's bluffs. And you can do this by learning what people's bodies are telling you, especially when they are trying to impress you. Their eyes can often tell you more than a résumé (which some service may have prepared for them). What people do with their feet while telling you about their management talents may tell you more than if you talked with them all day," he adds. "And smiles"—Wally's favorite topic—"are often like masks. People like to hide behind them," he quips (with a frown).

The main topic of Wally's seminar is really body language—how to read it and how to use it. Wally, of course, has the benefit of a great store of practical experience in "reading" people. But he also takes advantage of the science of kinesics, an area of research and theory which in the last twenty years has revealed many of the secrets of how we communicate with our facial expressions, our eyes, posture, hand gestures, the clothes we wear, and even our use of the space around us. Like Wally, you can put this science to work for you—not only in reading people more accurately, but in building your own communication power.

Wally's big joke is that each year it takes him five months to teach techniques that will often allow you to learn all you want to know in the first two minutes of an interview.

LEARN TO READ AND USE BODY LANGUAGE

Like most ambitious people, you have probably already thought about reading body language. You have noticed how people can appear insincere (shifty eyes, limp handshake), confident (looking you right in the eye, positive handshake, steady voice), or threatened (blushing, shaky hands, heavy breathing, squinty eyes). Although you've probably often been correct in your readings, you'll do better if you understand the larger scheme within which all body language seems to operate. One simple scheme is to distinguish among three levels of body language and the messages in each. These include: (1) basic emotions, (2) projected attitudes, and (3) language gestures.

WATCH FOR THE BASIC EMOTIONS

Pleasant-Unpleasant? Active-Dormant?

It's pretty clear that we humans come equipped with a set of basic emotions which are typically revealed first in our facial expressions and secondarily in our body positions and movements. Charles Darwin, in fact, studied these expressions as a part of his research into human evolution. Both Darwin as well as modern researchers have found that pictures of sad, surprised, sleepy, or mean faces are interpreted in much the same way by people of different cultures, from the Stone Age inhabitants of Borneo to Manhattan debutantes.

Facial expressions have also been used as a basis for developing psychological theories of human emotion. Mostly, the theories hold that our basic emotional state is a combination of feeling somewhere between pleasant and unpleasant, combined with feeling somewhere between the extremes of active and dormant.

> Analyze the first face that you can picture in your mind (someone in the room, a picture, a magazine ad, a face on TV). Where would this face fit on the pleasant-unpleasant scale and simultaneously on the active-dormant one? Take a few spare moments tomorrow and read some faces in terms of these two basic dimensions. What do they tell about the person's reactions to a given situation?

Degrees of pleasantness and activeness as indicators reflect fundamental psychological theory of how we humans, as well as most other animals, can be variously aroused (from dormant to some level of activeness) when presented with a stimulus, and how we evaluate that stimulus in terms of approach (pleasant) or avoidance (unpleasant). It is from these fundamental reactions that we develop our further, more complex emotions and attitudes.

> Imagine yourself as an actor trying to portray basic emotions of joy, anger, serenity, and hurt. Notice how each is developed from combinations of pleasantness-unpleasantness and activeness-passiveness. Tomorrow analyze the expressions on a few of the people around you (in the office, subway, or at the bank). What expressions are built up from the two basic dimensions? What do they tell you about how people are responding to their situations in terms of arousal and approach-avoidance?

Are Your Emotions Hanging Out?

Life for most of us is, of course, a daily trip through a variety of emotional states, from trying to get it all going in the morning to dropping off into a pleasant sleep at night. We may be happy, sad, surprised, or crushingly bored—all in the space of an hour. Our faces and bodies will typically show these differences, and we can read them in the people around us. But have you noticed how some people look perpetually happy, confused, bored, or just plain mean? In research that a colleague and I reported a number of years ago, we found that just as people can portray different emotions, they also carry around subtle perpetual expressions which may cause others to classify them in terms of general personality types. In other words, to a certain degree we all go around looking confident or confused, energetic or lethargic, pleasant or mean, and so on.

> Think of the people with whom you work. Do any of them carry around perpetual scowls? Who looks confident and why do you think this? Can you pick the "burned outs" in your midst? How do you think you look? (And while you're doing this, think of the great book title, *If I'm In Charge Here, Why Is Everybody Laughing?*)

We could go on at this point to concoct an elaborate chart of which body cues portray the basic emotions (as in eyes wide with surprise, etc.) but chances are excellent that if you are a normally functioning human being, you'll already know these cues well.

You have learned them by associating your own outward expressions with such inner feelings as joy, hate, or surprise. And because we humans are so similar in terms of these expressions, it is not difficult for you to expect to see them in others. With one great exception, you should find it relatively easy to recognize the cues of confidence, defensiveness, nervousness, suspicion, or admiration. The exception is that in nearly every culture there are strategies for disguising the basic emotions—the "stiff upper lip" strategy. We may try to look happy when we are basically sad, confident when we are unsure, or brave when we are scared stiff. This is called masking, and we'll discuss it later.

KNOW THE CUES OF PROJECTED ATTITUDES

Read Reactions

Our reactions to situations, of course, become more complex than simple approach-avoidance. Our mildly active unpleasant feelings may vary between such emotional—or more specifically attitudinal—reactions as frustration, anxiety, hostility, suspicion, or defensiveness. We can be pleasantly confident, feel sincere and exhibit a keen interest in a situation. Most such reactions are called "attitudes" because they reflect our disposition or manner of responding. We project these attitudes in our body language in ways that are often unique to our culture, or else our culture has taught us ways to suppress them.

> Think of the following projected attitudes which are often expressed in the body language of American and West European cultures. What are the cues of confidence, defiance, concern, openness, frustration, or sexual interest (male and female) in your society? What attitudes does your culture encourage you to suppress?

Remember that projected attitudes may vary considerably from culture to culture (as in Asian versus American) and even among subcultures (the young, the old; rural, urban). In most parts of the United States, holding your palms casually up in front of you and smiling slightly is a sign of openness. Rubbing the back of your neck, tugging at your collar, wiping your forehead, and hand wringing are signs of frustration. Folded arms and a feet-apart stance often indicate defiance. Cues of confidence include unyielding eye contact, assuming a relaxed posture in an important situation (e.g., sitting with your hands held behind your head), and "dismissal" (swishing your hand in front of you) or "emphasis" gestures (swinging your fist in front of you). We indicate concern by an extra-wide opening of our eyes, placing our hands out in front of us, and by mixed pleasant and inquisitive facial expressions.

Sex Cues

The sexual attitudes of a woman being addressed by a man are often shown in her posture (staying relaxed at first, not withdrawing or getting rigid). If the relationship progresses (even subconsciously), the woman may sit or stand more erect, elevating her breasts and maintaining close eye contact. (To a man, she will look more receptive.) A man responding sexually to a woman's addressing him will not stay relaxed, but will assume a more alert posture which itself addresses the woman. He, too, will strengthen eye contact, but may also explore her face and body with his eyes. Many of these processes can go on subconsciously, so that a one-way or mutual attraction may be underway before you sense it. (Or you may realize it after the encounter.) It is important to realize also that the outward expression of sexuality varies greatly from culture to culture.

Why are sexual cues so important now when considering your communication power? Simply because there are now many more women in executive positions, and sexual cues may either interfere with or enhance your communicative relationship with a member of the opposite sex (see Chapter 14). And they certainly make life more interesting!

How's Your Mask?

Finally, a word about masks. Often we try to develop tactics for disguising our projected attitudes. Some individuals who may in actuality be very nervous at a meeting may try to mask it by attempting to appear overly casual. A woman who wants to appear courteous to a man may smile and be attentive while her body defends itself with crossed legs and folded arms.

Masks are dangerous because we cannot always keep all of our projected cues under control. Slipped masks are a strong message of insincerity or lack of confidence. People will believe this interpretation no matter what you say in words.

In your next meeting (especially a boring one), study the projected attitudes of one of the participants. Look for masking behavior. Also, try to examine cross-sex communication in that same situation. Can you distinguish contrasts in male-female attraction? How much masking seems to be going on? Finally, what projected attitudes may dominate in your own body language?

LEARN THE LANGUAGE
OF GESTURES AND USE IT!

Communicate on
All Your Channels

Our emotions and projected attitudes influence how others will interpret what we say and do. Cues on this level are mixed between the conscious and subconscious. There are also gestures that we use much more consciously either to make a direct statement (pointing gestures = "The car is over there") or to give emphasis to what we say verbally (swinging fist in front of you = "I really mean it"). There is no clear line between gestures that we use for emphasis and many of the cues of projected attitudes discussed above. Many of them occur spontaneously as we speak. On the other hand, gestures that we substitute for words are much more intentional and may not come as naturally to you.

Most of us are already adept at reading language gestures in other people; therefore, our main task is to improve our own uses.

> Practice talking aloud about something that interests you—the more emotional and personal the better. Speak into a tape recorder and with nobody else present. Notice how you will try to gesture naturally even though there is no one there to impress. Then stand in the same empty room, but this time gesture outlandishly. Really overdo it. These exercises will give you a vivid sense of the natural gestures already in your repertoire. Your next task is to use them effectively, improving your timing, strength, and follow-through.

Many of our natural gestures are used to give emphasis to a verbal point. We may shift our hands down in front of us, nod our head, or move our body forward slightly as the point is spoken. If we are emphasizing our personal commitment or position in what we say, we typically gesture toward ourselves, often accompanied by a smile or expression of seriousness.

Give Your Gestures Strength
and Energy

The greatest problem most people have with their natural language gestures is failure to give them sufficient strength and energy. The cues are lifeless or restrained. (I call one version of this problem "fish gestures," as if your hands were coming out of the sides of your hips.) All the verbal power in the world can be compromised by halfhearted gestures. People will believe these gestures before the words. Another common problem is in getting your gestures slightly out of sync with the spoken emphasis. This promotes an image of awkwardness and artificiality, if not insincerity. (Sometimes I call this the "railroad signal" problem, as if the gesture is slowly coming on as the train approaches, but is just slightly out of correct timing.)

Lack of follow-through, like stopping your golf swing before its natural conclusion, also connotes awkwardness and is sometimes distracting. (This is the "fading fist" problem, where the hand goes up to gesture, we all wait for the point, then notice that the hand melts aways before anything important is said.) If you suffer from this problem, people will soon train themselves not to pay attention to your gestures at all, thus robbing you of a good 50 percent of your personal communication channel.

> Next time you speak in any situation, from a conversation to a board meeting, think about your natural gestures—not so much in terms of their content, but in terms of timing, strength, and follow-through. This point is worth putting on a note card in your briefcase.
>
> Have a videotape made of your oral speaking style. Analyze the strength and energy of your gestures. Just seeing yourself in action will help plenty. (This is the highlight of some thousand-dollar seminars in executive communication.) Chances are that someone in your company or organization has a videotape system that you can use on your own.
>
> For any presentation you are planning, make a special effort to consider how highly descriptive gestures could add clarity, power, and emphasis to what you say. Does your talk have three points? Count them out on your fingers. Can you "map" out a problem in terms of an imaginary layout which you describe with words and gestures? (Such images are more easily remembered than the words of a speech.) Can you describe shapes or levels with gestures? As with all gestures, timing, strength, and follow-through are essential. (If you are preparing for an especially important presentation, don't pass up practicing on videotape!)

THE BODY LANGUAGE OF SUCCESSFUL EXECUTIVES

Use Space to Your Advantage

Mr. M., the chairman of a large western banking chain, has an office that some of his associates jokingly refer to as his "throne room." If you were to enter this office, you'd be immediately struck by the imposing desk and immense high-backed executive chair that face down upon you from what looks like a city-block distance from the door. An expensive Persian carpet flows from the door not only right to the desk but under it and up the rear wall. Approaching Mr. M. in this imposing setting makes you realize what bringing tributes to an ancient pharaoh must have been like. But once you get to know him, you might observe how skillfully this Chief Executive Officer (CEO) uses his office space as a setting for not only powerful but varied communication. It sets the stage, so to speak, for his body language.

Without ever speaking a word, Mr. M. can communicate his authority over visitors. He can keep them waiting ever so slightly at his door until they are invited in. As there are no chairs immediately in front of his desk, you can be kept standing until he bids you to seat yourself. Then when you do sit, you may be restricted to an upright, hard-back chair (no relaxation invited here). He may feel free to answer his phone or intercom while you cool your heels. If his secretary stops in, he may talk to her while you wait again. He may even give you the "nonperson" treatment by talking about your visit in your presence.

Of course, Mr. M. isn't this much of a tyrant. He also has a couch and chairs on the side of his office. You could sit there and feel very comfortable. He might even sit on the opposite end of the couch from you and relax, with his hands behind his neck and a foot on the edge of the coffee table. His secretary could hold all phone calls and not disturb the two of you with either the intercom or a visit. You might even have a cup of coffee. And if you really knew Mr. M. well and it were late in the day, you might step into a side room where he has a few overstuffed lounge chairs and a wet bar.

The point in all this is to illustrate how body language in corporate ranks begins with your command over space. In one way or another we all play out our communication roles on a stage that is set by us or the other person. Use space to your advantage.

Use the Cues of Superior-Subordinate Relationships

If you are in management, you'll typically divide your time between roles of the superior-subordinate relationship. In the former you will want to command respect; in the latter you may want actively to convey it.

Set the stage clearly for your status relationship so you won't have to waste words on it. Take charge of the space if the territory is meant to be yours; respect it if it is the domain of your superior. Anticipate body-language cues that mark the superior-subordinate relationship. This does not mean that you place yourself in an oppressing or fawning relationship. It means that you are recognizing and operating within the established organizational structure.

Here are some strategies for communicating a status relationship from the superior's point of view. (Interpret the reverse if you want to carry out the subordinate's role.)

Position yourself so that it is natural for you to indicate where a subordinate is to sit when entering your office.

You can use a palm-downward handshake to connote a superior position (palm upward connotes respect).

Feel more free to point and to beckon than the subordinate.

As a superior, you can initiate a more relaxed posture or sitting position.

You decide what interruptions are to be tolerated. Too much interruption tends to put the subordinate in the "nonperson" role, which indicates either overt intimidation on the part of the superior or outright discourtesy.

In the superior's role, you have less obligation to maintain eye contact than does the subordinate (again, the "nonperson" situation could apply).

Territorial movement is more your prerogative as the superior, especially in movement toward or touching the desk.

The above characteristics of superior-subordinate relationships, although often disavowed or ridiculed by individuals who disagree with them, do continue to predominate in the organizations of the Western world. (I have also seen them even more evident in the supposedly classless societies of the socialist world. If you want to get along there, you observe these characteristics carefully but openly agree with all concerned that they do not exist.) These admittedly upper- to upper-middle-class attitudes occur in traditionally oriented organizations (which constitute most major businesses in the United States and Europe).

But there are exceptions. In high technology R & D (research and development) organizations, superior-subordinate relationships are not so overtly expressed. Individuals work more as project teams, and external symbols of status are intentionally suppressed. But more subtle ones do exist in terms of flexibility of working hours, choices of projects, "scut" work, and the tolerance of upper-level management to independence of ideas, work habits, and dress. The nature of the work force is changing. Technological workers like to think that they are on an increasingly equal footing with management. (At least two companies I know are calling their janitorial force "engineers" now. As you'd probably guess, the CEO's are former accountants!)

Employ the Characteristics of Confidence

We've already described confidence as a projected attitude. Obviously, it is especially important in the communication behaviors of the manager. An employee is best motivated when he or she believes that the supervisor or manager is a winner. Otherwise why should the employee trust his or her future to that person? Study after study indicates certain common characteristics that connote confidence. Many consist of body language.

To exhibit confidence, use clear, straightforward verbal communication accompanied by direct, energetic, well-synchronized gestures. Failure to back up verbal commands with appropriate body language is taken as a sign of weakness.

Make sure that your posture is erect.

Hand movements signifying confidence include chin stroking, as in thinking or reflection (especially when under fire), holding your hands out with palms down as if to say "Take it easy, things are under control," and "steepling" (fingers together like a church steeple).

It is a sign of confidence if you lack apparent masking. Or, put negatively, any cue that you are masking underlying emotion will immediately make your confidence suspect.

Standing with your hands behind your back or relaxing them behind your head while sitting is a sign of confidence.

Cues of lack of confidence include sweating, nervous hand movements, tics, or collar tugging.

Body Language in Selling, Negotiating, and Participatory Management

These executive behaviors often depend upon the success formula of communicating "confidence—yes, superiority—no."

> In selling, negotiating, or participatory management, try to combine cues of confidence with openness, but avoid cues of superiority. Show alertness, eye contact, and positive hand movements (e.g., openhandedness, palms up). Avoid excessive aggressiveness in control of space, pointing, or standing over an individual. Guard against revealing body cues of boredom or indifference when the other person is presenting ideas.

A key thought in selling, negotiating, or in sharing management planning is to seek conflict resolution rather than compliance in your communications. Try paying more attention to the other person as an individual rather than concentrating only upon his or her organizational role. Your reward will be getting the other person to act in ways that are mutually beneficial.

An overload of body cues of superiority can put you out of business in the selling game. And you'd never even get started as a negotiator in an organization where participatory management is stressed. Again, the formula: "Respect and authority—yes, dominance—no."

USE THE POWER OF BODY LANGUAGE!

By rough estimate, we only pay attention to about 10 to 20 percent of our nonverbal communications, yet according to some estimates, nonverbal communications dominate over 50 percent of our communications intake. You can easily improve your ability to "read" the body language of others as well as to make your own more effective. Such improvement only requires a few minutes a day. Use the time you are already spending in person-to-person communication to observe more closely the body language of others. And use this same time to improve your own techniques.

Get that extra 50 percent working for you!

17

Your Listening: Why Lend Anybody Your Ears?

Successful executives are often powerful listeners. They are not content to listen while another person rambles on. Rather, they know how to sift out what is important and they know what to do with it. You can improve your listening if you learn to employ a few of the psychological advantages available to every listener. Major companies are now paying tens of thousands of dollars to improve the listening skills of people who are on their way up in the managerial ranks. See what you can do for yourself by applying the simple strategies described in this chapter.

FOUR STEPS TO ACTIVE LISTENING

Most of us are not very good listeners. That doesn't mean that we fail to hear what's going on around us. It's rather that we fail to take advantage of the fact that our brains can listen at two to three times the speed that most people can talk. This time difference allows us to evaluate what the other person is saying; to edit out, underscore, and to organize what is important to remember. When we use this time difference to our advantage, we are engaging in active listening.

Ever get trapped in this one?

J.P.: I can't understand why our clerical costs are going through the ceiling these days. When my father started this business, he and my mother did their own paperwork. My dad got so good at bookkeeping that when he finally got around to hiring an accountant, he couldn't find one who knew as much as he did.

You: Right, J.P.! Cut clerical costs.

J.P.: It's the government that's done this to us. They are killing us with paperwork. Last week they wanted me to fill in some silly form about our employee rest rooms. They've even got us filling out paperwork on our paperwork. I don't know where it's all going to stop. Now get on it, and give me a progress report as soon as possible!

You: Right, J.P. Cut clerical costs.

Luckily, you did not get trapped, because you sifted out and responded to the key point in what was said.

> Use your time advantage over the speaker for your own purposes. Get to the heart of what that person is saying to you and begin to formulate your response.

Active listening keeps you in charge. There are four steps for putting active listening to work for your personal and professional benefit. They include:

1. Control and focus your attention.
2. Comprehend and structure what you hear.
3. Evaluate what you interpret.
4. Listen interactively.

Step One:
Control and Focus Your Attention

How Well Can You Focus Your Attention?
In a moment I'll ask you to close your eyes. When you do, I'd like you to do several things:

- Listen to the sounds about you.
- See if you can tune in to a few sounds that you're not aware of at this instant.

OK—close your eyes.

Did you hear anything in the background (office clatter . . . the air conditioner . . . talking . . . outside traffic . . . the TV or radio going . . . machinery . . . your refrigerator . . . the wind)? Unless you are reading this book in some kind of vacuum, you, like most of us, are engulfed in a world of sounds.

Probably far more than you have ever thought, you are listening every waking moment of your day. You cannot shut your ears the way you shut your eyes. It is only through mental concentration that you can survive in our modern, noisy environment. (Is your TV blatting away in the other room?) You can improve your power of concentration by practicing attention focusing.

How to Improve Your Attention Focus

Here are some simple exercises. They will give you some feel for the control process which you can carry over to practical situations of listening. Do them in your spare time.

> Get ready to close your eyes and concentrate on the sounds about you. When you close them, mentally list every sound you can identify. Then concentrate upon one which is not the closest or loudest to you. Try to describe it to yourself verbally ("deep hum, almost a rasping").
>
> Close your eyes and imagine the sounds of a siren, a doorbell, a plinking piano, and a dog barking.
>
> Turn on your radio or TV. Concentrate upon the number of times "the" is said in the next few minutes.
>
> The next time you speak with someone, make it a point to think about attention focus. While following what the other person is saying, try to see for yourself how much time is left over for you to think about what you are hearing.

Attention exercises work, and there are a multitude of them. Try making up some; use them when you might otherwise be wasting time, as in riding on the bus or plane, sitting through a long meeting, or sitting it out in your doctor's waiting room.

Focus With Your
Personal Motives Foremost

Have a personal purpose in how you listen. Perhaps you are at a business reception where your purpose is to mix with as many clients as possible. Focus your listening in each conversation so you can make a brief personal response and then move on.

Effective listening is not necessarily comprehending perfectly everything anybody says, but comprehending that which is important to you, that which suits your personal or professional needs.

> Think back to the most important conversation or meeting you had yesterday. Ask yourself: (1) How much did I concentrate upon what was important to me? (2) How much time was wasted with trivia or items not important to me? (3) How can I better use active listening to fulfill my personal or professional purpose next time?

Use Your Spare Time
in the Listening Process

As you take improved control over your attention focus in listening, use your time advantage over the speaker to engage in mental activities that will be beneficial to you.

> Don't let your listening rate slow down to the talker's speech rate. If you do, you'll be losing out on one of your most important advantages as a listener.

Whatever happens, don't stop listening while you try to puzzle over a word or problem. Instead, move on. Your biggest handicap as a listener is that you often cannot stop the speaker.

Use your spare time to concentrate on your basic comprehension and structuring of what you hear. These processes are at the heart of active and powerful listening. (They are discussed in the next section.)

Use the time differential to evaluate what you hear and to formulate your responses. Don't wait for your turn to think and talk. Plan ahead.

Having power over your focus of attention pays dividends far beyond the listening process. It works for everything from natural childbirth to speed-reading.

Step Two: Comprehend and Structure What You Hear

"Listening is like being handed one brick at a time and being expected to figure out what the house looks like." This complaint from a student is enlightening. Words do come to us in a one-by-one sequence, and it is in how we combine their meanings that we find out what the speaker is trying to say. In reading, we have the words all out in front of us. We can glance over whole sentences, even a paragraph, at once. We can go back to check on things. Or we can look ahead to see what is coming. But in listening, we are restricted to making our interpretations on the spot. Moreover, we want to extract from overall messages only those parts important to us. You can overcome these inherent handicaps as a listener by improving your skills at plain-sense comprehension and structuring.

Plain-sense comprehension is your ability to understand what is basically being said in word-to-word sequences. It is your internal understanding of individual words and sentences.

Structuring is your ability to put together what you hear into ideas and the overall message. Structuring is understanding the whole point that the other person is trying to express.

You can usually improve both skills by applying the following strategies.

Anticipate Key Words and Structure

Not every word in the language sequence is important for the meaning of the message. As you read the following passage, mentally fill in the missing words.

"Look, I'll _____ four hundred more this afternoon. _____ I can phone it _____, we'll probably get delivery _____ no later than noon _____. Now will that be _____ enough for you to _____ up on the Witkins _____ or not?"

Many of the missing words came easily, didn't they? This was not because I deleted only trivial words; indeed, the pattern was to delete every fifth one after randomly selecting a starting place.

Our spoken language is so redundant that about 20 percent of it can be deleted and we can still get the meaning of the message. Most of the message above can be gleaned from the overall context rather than individual words. There are only four key words in the entire passage—*four hundred, noon, tomorrow,* and *Witkins.* (For the missing words, see below.*) The most effective plain-sense listening strategy is to listen carefully for these key words and to remember their precise meanings. The remainder of the words will contribute only to the general context of these meanings and do not require your primary attention.

> Anticipate types of key words that are likely to appear in what you hear. Get ready to interpret their specific meanings. Plan ahead as to which key words are important for your personal purposes in listening to someone.
>
> Ask an office colleague a question that will require several hundred words to answer. Think of which key words will probably appear in the response. Now listen for these words and notice how they stand out if you anticipate them.

Plain-sense comprehension is sometimes hampered by words that we may not immediately understand. However, if you pay close attention to their immediate contexts, you can often deduce meanings. Consider these sentences:

> The sail flapped because of the broken *burton.*
> The Model III computer holds twice the *bytes* of the Model II.
> Most of the *variance* is in cost overruns.
> The *rho* of +.89 shows job effectiveness and training closely related.

> If you encounter key words that are unintelligible to you, don't stop the listening process because of them. Try to generate meanings from their immediate context. Have a friend or family member select a dozen or so rare or technical words from a dictionary. Based upon the definitions given, have them include each word in a sentence. Listen to (or read) the sentences and try to generate the key word meanings from immediate contexts.

Now go back to the above example and guess the meanings of the capitalized words from their immediate contexts. (Check your answers below.**)

We also generate meanings from the overall context of a message. Sometimes the details take on a very different meaning as we understand the larger theme. Suppose that you heard the following spoken very quickly:

---

*Look, I'll *order* four hundred more this afternoon. *If* I can phone it *in,* we'll probably get delivery *by* no later than noon *tomorrow.* Now will that be *soon* enough for you to *finish* up on the Witkins *order* or not?

**A *burton* is part of the rigging of pulleys. A *byte* is a unit of computer information. *Variance* is the deviation of cost figures from the predicted figures. *Rho* is a statistical index of correlation between two sets of measures.

No matter how inadequate we might feel when we arrived, we wouldn't feel guilty about it, nor would we feel that there was nothing we ourselves could do for we would have gone armed with all kinds of resources as well as the belief that we would improve our knowledge of the language, our understanding of the people, and that we would grow steadily in our ability not simply to live in an entirely foreign culture but to enjoy it.

The details in this passage make sense as is. Who wrote it? An explorer? A world traveler? Maybe Marco Polo? Well, it's a selection about women moving into a male-dominated management world. (If you would like to read the whole selection, you'll find it on page 186 in *The Managerial Woman* by Margaret Hennig and Anne Jardim, Anchor Press/Doubleday, 1977.)*

Anticipate the overall theme of what a person is saying to you. What is the speaker's purpose and what do the details mean relative to that purpose? If the overall theme isn't soon clear to you, you are wasting your time. You will not have the necessary basis for interpreting details. Ask questions or tune out. Ambiguity isn't worth it. In fact, it's dangerous.

Assert Your Hearing
and Questioning Rights as a Listener

Have you noticed how some people will sit passively when it is perfectly obvious that they do not understand what they have heard? Or have you seen people sitting in the back rows of an auditorium where they couldn't possibly hear half of what is going on? (And remember that PA systems break down more than the laws of chance should allow!)

Don't put up with not being able to hear. Move in closer. Stand up and ask for the speaker to speak a little louder or to get closer to the mike. (I'd estimate that about 25 percent of all listening problems come from poor acoustics, faulty mikes, and soft-voiced speakers—combined with listeners who are too timid to exercise their rights.)

Basic questions for the benefit of plain-sense comprehension are fair game. Obviously most ministers are not ready for us to stand up in the middle of their sermons and ask for a definition of "grace," nor do we get very far in talking back to the CEO at a board meeting. Yet there are many situations when people could ask clarifying questions, but shrink back out of shyness or a false sense of impropriety. If you pass up these opportunities and lose out on what's said, it's your fault. Questions can be asked politely and unobtrusively.

If key words or overall theme are unclear to you, listening failure will be at your expense unless you ask questions. Pose them in clarifying rather than threatening styles. ("When you say *productivity,* do you mean mainly *profit?*"

---

*Excerpt from *The Managerial Woman* by Margaret Hennig and Anne Jardim. Copyright © 1976, 1977 by Margaret Hennig and Anne Jardim. Reprinted by permission of Doubleday & Company, Inc., and Marion Boyers Ltd., London.

"What's the name of that city again . . . Tallahassee?" "Could you spell that term again, please?"

Visualize Meanings

We may hear words but we comprehend meanings. The more we can visualize most meanings, the more efficient will be our interpretations of individual key words. There are many memory techniques that will aid your visualization and retention processes (see Chapter 20).

Sharpen your powers of mental visualization. The next time you hear the TV news, close your eyes and visualize as vividly as possible the key meanings for what you hear. Open your eyes from time to time to see how your visualizations correspond with the TV image. Consciously visualize the next time you are in any listening situation of a few minutes or more, especially a talk or a meeting. The more vivid the image to you, and often the more unusual, the better you will remember it.

Use Devices
for Structuring What You Hear

Mental structuring is a key to comprehension. The more visual are your techniques for structuring meanings, the better you will remember what you hear.

Anticipate the overall structure of what you are about to hear. Will it fit into some type of outline, diagram, or vivid mental visualization?

Caution against copious note taking because it will interfere with the listening process. (It will take away from the time you have to think about what you are hearing.) The best notes are ones that contain only key words or materials which will jog your memory. One efficient tactic is to take only very simple notes while you are listening, then, at a later time, write or dictate a more complete version.

Step Three:
Evaluate What You Hear

Examine Motives as You Listen

Use your time advantage over the speaker to evaluate what you hear. Use the steps in the motivating sequence (H3W in Chapter 6) to ask yourself questions like the following:

What am I being asked to do? If it isn't clear, what are they leading up to? Am I sure that I am thinking about the same *what* as they are? Is the *what* more complicated than it appears on the surface? How can I get the *what* more in line with my interests?

Why am I being asked to do it? Is it something that fulfills my motives? What are the other person's motives? Do they conflict with mine (the "you lose, I win" game)? Are there deeper motives involved which might be contrary to what I think is going on here? Am I falling prey to motives for which I'm a pushover? Am I kidding myself? Are the other person's reasons sound? Facts correct? What kind of person is asking this of me?

When am I supposed to do this? If right now, will it be to my advantage or the other person's? Can I or should I have more time to think about it? Should I get more facts and opinions? If the *when* isn't clear, why? Can I have the *when* on my schedule, not theirs?

Hey—why am I listening to all this? Is it important? Should I bow out or tune out fast? Should I give this thing more attention? Am I getting my "two cents' worth"? Is the other person paying any attention to me? Am I just getting grabbed by the *hey!* pitch?

Look Actively for the Positive

The route to positive communications is not found in just avoiding the negative. You must actively seek the positive. Even the term *evaluate* means to seek the value in something. Avoiding the negative without seeking the positive could leave you with but one result—the mediocre.

> Look for motives that are positive—that is, those qualities sought by normally healthy and strong people. These motives have more to do with psychological growth than with physical security. They are "you win-I win" games. They include appeals to clear definitions of reality, positive concepts of self, the ability to see things objectively, new and open experiences, spontaneity, expressiveness, creativity, love—all of those qualities that make us feel more fully human. These are the signs of valuable communication for you.
>
> Look for positive qualities in the communications structure. Is it factual, logically reasoned, and well balanced? Does it include expert opinion? Does it respect your motives and opinions? If so, it is valuable to you.
>
> Look for positive qualities in the speaker. These include honesty, sincerity, credentials, and a respect for you as an individual. If you cannot find these qualities, question the communications.

Step Four: Increase
Your Interactive Listening Skills

The Germans have a phrase for it and it's a mouthful: *aneinander vorbeireden.* It means "talking past somebody"—not responding, but still talking. We do it too often.

Supervisor: People are getting too careless in answering the phone here. Pick it up on the first ring.

Employee I: But sometimes we're not sure who is supposed to answer it.

Supervisor: After saying "Good Morning" or "Good Afternoon," give the company name, then your name. . . .

Employee II: Sometimes I can't take a second call.

Supervisor: Try to handle requests yourselves or give a reason if you have to transfer the caller.

If we listened as conscientiously in our give-and-take with others as we concentrated on talking, communication would go on at a much more effective level in most organizations.

If we drew a diagram of it, *aneinander vorbeireden* would look something like this:

```
_____
                              >>>>>>>>>>>>>>>>>>>>>>>
        YOU

_____        _____


                                                      THEM

                                _____
```

Truly effective two-way listening would look like this:

```
_____—>>>>>>>>>>>—_____
        YOU                                   THEM
_____—<<<<<<<<<<<—_____
```

This is interactive listening. The goal is to gain convergence of meanings, to bring you and the speaker together. That's the same meaning as is associated with the historical root of the word *Communicate*—i.e., "to bring together."

Following are four practical suggestions for improving your interactive listening skills.

Actively Check on What You Interpret

Go for convergence with the speaker. Use your turn to talk as a basis for verifying what you have just heard, the conclusions you're drawing, or any important implications.

> Try direct paraphrases on the plain-sense-comprehension level. ("Let's see if I got it right . . ." or "You mean . . .") When you try this, notice that it will often tune in the speaker. The other person will start thinking of what he or she says in terms of how you may paraphrase it.
>
> Test your structuring. See if the mental map in your head resembles the one in the speaker's. ("There were three points, right?" "The main reason for selling these out is . . .")
>
> Ask a provocative question. Get other people to test their own structuring. Put them on notice that you are not only following them, but also evaluating. ("Isn't there really a fourth reason in addition to those you've given?" "What happens if you don't make a profit?")

Make Direct Tests of Motives

Motives are, after all, your reasons for wanting to communicate. Check them.

> Make a direct test of the *why*. There may be more to consider here than the other person's or your direct motives. There is also what you think the other person has in mind, as well as what he or she thinks about you. These may differ from the actual motives. ("Frankly, Phil, why do you want *me* to be the one to do it?" "Look, I am mainly in this to get the market exposure; what's in it for you?") Seek common ground in your interactions on motives. How can you both win?

Accentuate the Positive

If you and the speaker accomplish something positive, you will both have a greater chance for a "win" in the long run.

> Try to redirect any give-and-take that begins to move in a negative direction. ("Wait, why don't we see if we can do this without both of us being taken to the cleaners?")
> Praise works better than blame. ("Well, I can't accept your offer, but I appreciate your trying to do well by me.") Give other people any credit they deserve, maybe a little bit even if they don't deserve it. Try for "you win-I win" convergence in your interactions.

Use Silence Productively

Learn to tolerate silence as a listener so you are not forced into premature responses. Silence itself communicates.

> Try *not* saying something now and then. You'll see that it has positive effects. If other people are unloading on you, let them go ahead and get it out of their systems. The chances are good that their emotions are so worked up that they will not hear anything positive you say to them short of "uh huh." (And they may even hear that as "no.")

LISTENING STRATEGIES WILL WORK FOR YOU

Don't try to do all these suggestions at once. In fact, you'll probably never get around to using all of them. You'll be most successful with them if you try one or two at a time.

Some of these suggestions—especially the attention-focus exercises—are easily practiced in your spare time. The comprehension and structuring suggestions can be practiced during boring meetings.

Sharpen your skills with these ideas in low-risk situations. Then when you are doing some important listening, they will be at your disposal.

And there is a final dividend in effective listening: It is half the art of effective conversation!

18

Your Reading:
Why Evelyn Wood
Made a Million

(Jot the time down in the margin. We'll refer to it later.)

> How can you keep a clean desk when there is more to read—letters, documents, professional journals—than you have time? The answer is simple. You can develop a strategy called executive speed-reading. You can easily cut in half the time you now spend reading by being more selective in what you read, the rate at which you scan the text, and by reading with your personal and professional objectives foremost in mind. (How long has it taken you to read this opening paragraph? If longer than ten seconds, you have room for improvement.)

WHY READING BOGS US DOWN

Reading is one of the most unnatural and complex behaviors we humans force ourselves to do. The written language is only an imperfect notation of our natural, spoken language. We can think much faster than we can read. We readers are at the mercy of the clarity and organization of the writer. Moreover, many of us have learned to read in especially cumbersome and inefficient ways. It is no wonder that there are large segments of our population who read very little, if at all. Nor is it surprising how our desks and in-baskets become crammed with more material than we think we can read or even how some of our favorite magazines lie at home unread for lack of time.

Sylvia F. had an unexpected problem when she was starting out in a bank management training program after college graduation. About six months into the job, Sylvia was ready not only to drop her executive aspirations but to drop out of city life, too ("to find a little valley where she could macramé Volkswagens," as she put it). Sylvia simply could not keep up with her reading although, as she explained, she had conscientiously read every important report "word by word" and was taking home financial magazines to sift through night after night. Almost totally by accident, Sylvia got the idea of taking a speedreading course when her doctor told her that she had taken one as the only way she could keep up with her medical journals.

Sylvia signed up at the local community college for a short speedreading course, although that seemed a little odd to her as a former honors student. But at the first night's class Sylvia discovered her reading problem, cured it in a few days' practice, and within a week had nearly quadrupled her reading speed.

Although Sylvia was surprised when she found out the nature of her problem, it was not really an unusual one. She was a "subvocalizer." After years of reading aloud in primary school classes, she had carried over to her silent reading a tendency to murmur many of the words she read. This kept her average reading speed at about 125 words per minute, a speed about one-fourth an average effective silent reading rate.

Although chances are that you do not have a problem like Sylvia's, you still can benefit greatly by attempting to improve your reading efficiency— that is, to get more out of what you choose to read and to spend less time getting it. There are strategies that seem to work particularly well for persons who are literally faced with more reading than their schedule allows or who want to improve their comprehension and efficiency with the reading they do now. I call these the strategies for executive speed-reading.

A FOUR-PART STRATEGY FOR EXECUTIVE SPEED-READING

Take the next fifteen to twenty minutes and learn the parts to this strategy. Before you put the book aside today, test your speed on one of the sections identified at the end of this chapter. Then apply these strategies as much as possible in your personal and professional reading. One month from today, test yourself again on a section identified at the end of this chapter. See how much you have improved.

As a preview, the four-part strategy includes:

1. Know what you want from what you read.
2. Know where to find what you want.
3. Employ "search-read" tactics.
4. Know what to do with what you find.

OK—here are the strategies.

1. Know What You Want From What You Read

What's My Purpose?

Very little of the time we spend with reports, papers, magazines, and books could be justified if we read absolutely aimlessly. It is also true that most of us do read with one purpose or another in mind. The critical problem is that we do not make the purpose sufficiently precise, nor do we keep it at a sufficiently conscious level when we read. Instead, we are lulled into reading more than we need to in order to achieve our purpose. If we read without a purpose, we may often find ourselves daydreaming. Worse, we are drawn into reading mostly what the author wants us to see, not what we may personally need.

> Identify your specific purpose for reading any materials with which you may spend more than five minutes. Develop the attitude that you want a guaranteed return on your time investment in reading anything (including your morning paper).

Be in Charge of What You Read

Remember that *your* purpose is to be served. You may only want to see objective evidence of a company's profitability. Yet the author of the annual report may want you to see growth potential while the profit-loss statement is tucked away in fine print. Read with personal purpose and keep conscious of this purpose. (Otherwise, how will you know when to stop? Hopefully you won't have to read to the end.)

> Keep your anticipated time investment at a conscious level. Are you willing to make a bigger investment if it's taking more time to get what you need? How much is too much? (How much time have you wasted searching for something that wasn't there or was hidden? Why not have a cutoff point?) Again, remember that it is *your* purpose and *your* time.

2. Know Where to Find What You Want

Look for Your Payoff!

The biggest mistake you can make is to read a document word by word, page by page, through to its end. (If you had a list of ten places a treasure might be buried off the Bahamas, you wouldn't go down that list place by place, would you? No. If you were smart, you'd go first to the place where you think the probability of finding what you want is the greatest.) It's the same with reading. The more you can figure ahead of time where you can find what you want, the more time you'll save.

Never start reading until you know where to look for what you want. Does the letter, document, or publication have a format that you can use as a map for moving directly to what you are looking for? Does the writer have a clear method for organizing content? Don't assume that the writer is always that eager to give you what you want. You may have to dig it out. Going directly to the conclusions of a report, then working your way back to details (if necessary), will often save you time.

Almost any publication series has a recurring format imposed by its editor. The better you know that format, the more efficiently you can skip the trivia and move directly to what you want. (Ever notice how an experienced director of a company can pull the basic figures out of an annual report, no matter how glossy it is?) Often what you want is hidden in gobbledygook or small print, or it's tucked away in some small corner of a report. Many times, you must look for "obvious opposites" and expect them to be hidden. Ever notice how unintelligible a written guarantee can be, or a legal contract?

Don't Be Fooled

Sometimes a writer will use bait to draw your attention away from a particular point. (A project report I once reviewed extolled the "warm, human and personal" qualities of a local TV show which the federal government had sponsored as an experiment in getting poor people jobs. The dozen or so personal testimonials they included in their report almost completely overshadowed the hard fact that they had spent about forty thousand dollars, and only six people had gotten jobs that they had stayed in longer than a week!) Look out for bait even in short letters. ("We enjoyed your seminar documents immensely. They are truly outstanding! Although we are not in a position to purchase your services now—and thus we have cancelled payment on our earnest-money check—we will certainly be back in touch." The plain fact is that they photocopied the materials.)

If you must dig out what you need from a longer report or book, remember that an index is almost always more objective than a table of contents. The former is usually prepared by an unbiased clerk, while the latter will have all the biases of the report's author. Beginnings and especially endings of publications, when skimmed, may reveal much about internal structure. For quantitative materials, you can almost always expect tables. (In the worlds of science or finance, you can almost always go directly to summary tables of results.)

A rapid, "thumb-through" analysis of the format and content of headings in a document is often an efficient basis for locating key items.

In short, know where you're going before you begin reading. For anything except letters, what you want is almost never on the first page, so why start reading in detail there? For letters, if it isn't on the first page, it might not be important enough to worry about!

3. Employ "Search-Read" Tactics

Once you know the layout of the document or book, you start the process of "search reading." The "search" part means that you do not start reading in detail until you have found what you are looking for. It is the scanning or skimming part of the process. The "read" part means that you move to a level of detailed reading. This is a slower process, but you can still speed it up and even improve comprehension with a few strategies. The search-read process involves going back and forth between scanning and focusing (concentrating) reading until you have fulfilled your purpose in reading the material.

Search Before Reading

Search means that you *do not* let yourself get trapped into reading in any more detail than you need to determine where you are or where you are going in the materials. This is a scanning or skimming skill. It can involve reading headings, skimming tables, or referring back and forth to the index and the text. You are using search skills when you glance over the newspaper, looking only for items that interest you. You also use them with the telephone directory, a catalog, a dictionary, or a recipe book. The more you know about layout, the more efficient will be your search process.

> Consciously think about searching rather than reading whenever you pick up a letter, document, or book. Think about your purpose and how much time it's worth to fulfill that purpose. Then use what you have learned about the layout of the materials as an advanced organizer for your search. Look for key words or figures. Look for the gist, or kernel statements of your desired subject matter. Search is as much a state of mind as it is a skill. Do not let yourself read until you have what you want.

Know When to Read

When you think that you have hit pay dirt, then you'll want to read. This means getting the information off of the page and into your head in the most rapid yet accurate manner. But as soon as you have all that you need from where you are reading, start searching again. Don't get bogged down.

Improve Your Basic Reading Speed

Quick-check your basic reading speed. (If you read this chapter from the beginning, you have now read 2,250 words. Divide this by the number of minutes you have spent. For more tests, go to the end of this chapter.) If you are in the 200 to 300 words-per-minute range, you are reading relatively normally, but slower than need be for this type of material. If you want some strategies for speeding up your basic reading process, continue to the next paragraph. If you are OK for now, skip ahead to the next strategy (number 4).

If you are reading slowly (say, under 150 wpm), immediately check yourself for subvocalization problems.

Select another page randomly in any other chapter of this book. As you read, place your fingers lightly on your throat. Can you feel a vibration? Are you vocalizing slightly? Are your lips moving slightly? If either, try consciously to avoid this habit. You can start by forcing yourself to count aloud softly while reading. This will put your voice and lips to work on something other than your reading. It will also make you very conscious of how silent reading and motions of your vocal cords and lips can be made independent of one another. (If counting is too confusing, try saying "duh, duh, duh . . .") Practice this now and then for about five minutes at a time over a week. If your reading speed does not pick up, consult with an expert. (Look in the Yellow Pages under "Schools." Or call the education department at a local college or university.)

If you are reading more slowly than you wish and you suspect that the problem is your failure to see more than one or two words at a glance, then try some techniques to expand your perceptual unit.

Cut out a column of a newspaper article. Then further cut the column into blocks of text about one-half-inch long and paste each block on a three-by-five-inch card. (About ten will do.) With the blocks in their original order, "flash" them to yourself for a duration just long enough for you to get the essential meaning of what is written in each. (Skip sentences that have been cut off in the middle.) Try as much as possible to see the text as a unit rather than word by word. Practice this with other text samples and try to flash the cards faster each time.

Take a page in this book or any other and divide it vertically into three columns of equal width. (You can do this by bringing the outside edge in about two thirds of the way across the page, then folding the page vertically at that point and at the fold where the page is bent over. Or you can measure and draw lines if you wish.) Fold the page back out so you can see its three columns. Try to read this page by looking directly at the center column and only peripherally at the two outside ones. Instead of moving your eyes line by line, try to zigzag or swirl them rapidly down the center column. Keep practicing this. You'll begin to feel the difference if you are getting better at perceiving larger blocks of text. Check your speed improvement if you wish. (If you used the folded-page approach, try reading only the center column with the outer columns folded out of sight. Notice how much meaning you can still get from the reading. Or better yet, think of how much text upon which you have been wasting your time!)

There are many other techniques for improving your basic reading speed. You'll find them in the many books on the subject or in a local course on speed-reading. Most people will save more overall time by use of the search tactics than by speeding up their basic reading process. But together, they can take you to the five-thousand-plus words-per-minute level and give you the feeling of power that comes with mastery of the printed page!

4. Know What to Do With What You Find

Another problem that bogs us down, especially in our professional reading, is the lack of a plan for remembering what we read—or sometimes deciding what we do not want to remember.

Remember, File, or Index?

Plan ahead whether you want to remember, to file, or only to index what you read.

> If your goal is to remember, be prepared to employ memory techniques, highlighting, and note-taking strategies. If you have things important enough to you to file, then you had better have a filing system set up or your desk will become more cluttered than ever. Bear in mind that you have the third alternative of indexing. All you need is a note system that will tell you where to find the materials when you want them. Most of us could benefit from more indexing and less filing.

Use Memory Aids

Many of the memory techniques described in Chapter 20 are also found in courses on speed-reading. The tactic is to have an anticipated "memory format" for what you read. This can vary from a mental outline that you fill in as you read, to a method for constructing visualizations. The latter are mental images, sometimes bizarre ones, that combine cues for what you wish to remember. (Our visual memory is much more powerful than our verbal one.)

One very useful memory device or note-taking format for remembering the pros and cons of an issue is the accountant's *T*. Think of a page divided down the middle and with a line across the top. On the right you put notes on the pro side of an issue; on the left, the cons. As you read, fill in the two sides. (This is also an effective device for summarizing a sales presentation to a client.)

Key-word acronyms are also helpful memory tools. For each major point you wish to remember, peg it with a key word. Then put the first letters of those words together to form an easily remembered acronym. (For example, the four parts of the executive speed-reading strategy can be reduced to the key words *Purpose, Organization, Search,* and *Save.* Remember *POSS,* which will also remind you of a *positive* use of your reading time, and you'll probably remember the four parts. See Chapter 20 for more of these.)

Don't assume that the author's organizational outline will be the best mental or note-taking outline for you. Put your outline into a form targeted to your purpose for doing the reading in the first place. Make the materials work for you!

Have An Idea File

Consider setting up an idea file to serve both your indexing and filing needs. This works best if it is a regular part of a secretary's responsibilities to keep the file in order. Work up a set of regular categories, including such possible extras as "new thoughts," "items to look into later," or "UBI's" (unfileable but interesting!).

> Use your idea file to keep track of clippings, photocopied items, and jottings. Mark the clippings by category so there is no problem in filing them. For any item longer than a few hundred words, consider highlighting (using a very light yellow felt-tip pen) the key points before filing. Once a year, close out the file and start a fresh one.

Don't try to get everything in the file. Many items may be worth only an indexing—that is, a note on where the information can be found if you should ever want it. The secret to an idea file is to make it a matter of habit. Make yourself do the clipping and jotting, and be sure items get filed. You'll end up spending less time doing this than you would in keeping track of everything you saved to read but never got around to. Try never to leave anything on your desk for more than one day. (If you don't get it marked or filed, then it may not be important enough!) Try this at home, too, and see if you can't then throw out all those old magazines you wanted to get back to.

REAP SOME NEW BENEFITS

If you employ the strategy of executive speed-reading, you'll notice a few extra dividends. One is a cleaner desk. Think about it—isn't most of what's piled up on your desk simply things you haven't gotten around to reading or don't want to spend the time on?

Another benefit is an increased level of consciousness of time and purpose in reading. Very soon you'll be even more aware that more material comes to your desk than is really necessary.

You'll feel some dividends, too, when you set out to write your next report. The more you write with purpose and keep that purpose out front in the organization of your materials, the better will be your chance of communicating it clearly to another person.

Finally, you should reap the one great added benefit that was another positive conclusion to the Sylvia W. Story. After tripling her average reading speed, Sylvia found a whole new world of reading for pleasure open to her.

Reading-improvement strategies do work. That's how Evelyn Wood made her mark.

CHECK YOUR READING SPEED

Below are ten samples selected for you from different sections of this book. They are all of average difficulty. Use one or two to gauge your speed now. Save the remainder for subsequent tests. Return to all for retests, but remember that you will also be increasing your speed because the materials will be more familiar to you on second and third readings. Mark the beginning and ending before you start to read. All beginnings are at page tops, endings at page bottoms. Consciously set a goal for yourself of doubling your speed each month until you have reached a level at which you feel a sense of command and power in your reading.

Page	to	Page	Approx. Words	Time	Speed	Date
13		15	1,250			
23		27	1,875			
35		39	2,250			
48		49	1,000			
51		53	1,250			
57		62	2,500			
74		75	750			
81		83	1,400			
91		95	2,300			
114		121	3,750			

19

Your Writing:
It's Not What
They Taught You

If you're like most executives, the bulk of your writing is business correspondence. Chances are that your problem is not so much how to get the first sentence down, but how to keep the paperwork moving. Your first step for getting on top of this problem is to cut your correspondence load—maybe up to 50 percent. You do this not only by writing fewer letters, but shorter ones. Your other writing chores probably involve documents and reports. This is where getting the first sentence down can be a chore. How about not trying to start with the first sentence, but employing a four-step strategy designed to bypass hassles and to turn out documents on which you are proud to put your name? It will be a far cry from what they taught you in school about writing, but it works!

LETTER LITTER

To: All Department Heads
Fr: J. John P., Administrative Officer
Subj: Standard Operating Procedures

It has come to my attention during my first two months here that our standard operating procedures are not being followed by department heads in setting working hours as well as days off. It is apparent to me, too, that smoking rules are being flagrantly violated. Although I realize that these procedures have not been reviewed for some time, it is also the case that there has been no authorization to bypass them.

Let's all put our shoulders to the wheel and show that we can follow regulations!

J.J.P.

Mr. Harold K., Sales Manager
KMX Tape Company
Johnstonville, Wis.

Dear Mr. K.,

Please send us your wholesale catalog and price lists on the new line you introduced last week.

Yours truly,
Roland J.

Ms. Mildred F.
116 Shady Nook Lane
P.V. Calif., 91117

Dear Ms. F.,

I must bring to your attention again that we have a special program of assessments which were due at the close of the last fiscal year.

Although I can appreciate your concern as expressed in your letter of 1 Oct. with having to be assessed this fiscal year for city expenses authorized under Article 123.77 of the county code, the charges for the next fiscal year are included in the Form 26A recently sent to you. These disbursements are allocated on a quarterly basis such that the neighborhoods in Tracts 30000.1 through 40000.2 will only pay triannually. Again, therefore, the charges are transferable to you as the legal assignee.

This is our third notice.

Sincerely,
Franklin J.,
Fiscal Officer

None of the above letters is outlandishly off the mark, but each is representative of the daily inefficiencies we put up with in our correspondence. You can probably already guess that J. John P. didn't last the year as the new administrative officer. His memos were put-downs which did not invite understanding and cooperation. They were as phony as he was. Although Roland J. was not a phony—he really was in the retail tape business—it took three exchanges of letters before the KMX Tape Company knew exactly what he wanted and felt safe enough to reveal a few wholesale prices to him. Although fiscal officer Franklin J. was trying to be exact and courteous, about a week later he learned that he had totally failed to communicate. This came in the form of a sweet note on flowered stationery from Ms. J., a retired lady of seventy-five, saying:

> Dear Mr. K.,
>
> Thank you so much for your understanding. I knew you would agree that I should not be assessed again this year.
>
> God bless you,
> Mildred J.

It finally took Mr. K. a phone call to cut through his own written "bureaucratese" and to say what he really meant.

THREE STEPS FOR GETTING AHEAD IN THE CORRESPONDENCE GAME

We live in a world of paper shuffling, and our business correspondence is no exception. This is ironic, because business correspondence should be the most simple of all writing. All we need strive for is clarity. We're not looking for literary masterpieces or impressive verbiage. All we want is for another person to know or do something. It's just that simple, but somehow letter-writing conventions have made our correspondence all too complex and cumbersome. If your own day is bogged down with correspondence problems, try these three strategies:

1. Cut your correspondence load.
2. Write short letters.
3. Write only for results.

Step One: Cut Your Correspondence Load

Most executives—especially harried ones—handle too much mail. How well organized is your office?

> Go in to work early tomorrow or go in Saturday morning and take at least one uninterrupted hour to analyze your correspondence routines—both in and out. Ask:
>
> A. How many letters could be screened by another office and handled before they ever get to you? (And which do not need to get to you?)
>
> B. How many letters could your secretary automatically handle if you had a routine set up for them (including standard response formats)?
>
> C. How many letters could be answered with a simple telephone call by you or your secretary, including only a message left with the other party's office?

D. How many letters could be sorted into a stack so you could dictate brief answers which your secretary could translate into letter form (and maybe you'd never have to see again)?

E. Could you sort your mail into priority categories so you put off dull and unimportant matters to handle during those late-afternoon, uncreative periods of your week (or perhaps the matter might even eventually take care of itself)? This frees you to do your critical correspondence in your prime intellectual and emotional periods of the workday.

In other words, get a routine going. And don't start answering your mail when you go in early tomorrow until you've got the routine figured out!

Business theorists tell us that organizations themselves are big communications games. The team hierarchy of management is designed to handle routine matters on the lower levels so as to save upper-level executives for the critical decision making. So if you are a prisoner of routine correspondence, you're playing a losing role in the organization game. Get out of it before they take you out!

Step Two:
Write Shorter Letters

Not only in our offices but in our homes we are glutted with more communication than we can ever hope to assimilate. As a consequence, we learn to scan what is thrust into our attention and to only interpret as much of it as we need to get the main point. We throw out most of our junk mail without ever opening it because a third-class mailing frank and a cheaply printed envelope tell us it isn't worth looking at. Or we skim the first page of a letter only so far as we need to get the main point. If we can't get the point pretty fast in a long letter and it doesn't seem to be from anybody who is important to us, we dump it.

Neither should we expect others to comb through long letters of our own to find the point.

Never write a business letter longer than one page. (Sure, there are exceptions to this, but try to avoid them.) If you must include details, put them into an enclosure. Save space by omitting redundant and trite openings and closings ("Good to hear from you" or "Thank you again for writing"). Focus everything on your main point. Letters that have a single main point are typically the most effective. Get to the main point clearly and early in your letter. And it doesn't hurt to summarize it again in the closing. In short, write short!

Think of modern letters as messages rather than as long expositions. If you have some extended narrative to convey, put it into document form, with the key point for action in a cover letter. Then telephone to insure that the other person received it and understood it. If a narrative is critically important, go see the client personally and make an oral presentation. Sometimes an accompanying illustration, chart, or table will save you pages of words. Feel free to include a simple sketch in a one-page letter.

If you want some samples of forms to use for routine letters, consult a book on the topic (there are many; the best will probably be in your local library). But if you adopt a form letter, see if you can shorten it. You might even consider pretesting it on some folks in the office to be sure that the point gets across.

Lists and other forms of enumeration allow you to cut transition verbiage (e.g., "Let's (1) send the shipment, (2) bill them collect, and (3) expect payment in 45 days.")

Consider replacing your usual short letters with personal notes or message forms. A very brief note, handwritten or typed informally by you on personalized half-size stationery, is particularly effective for acknowledgments, a message to enclose with a mailing, or for confirmation of a meeting. There are a variety of message forms available from stationery companies which can be printed to order with your logo. Personal notes are modern, effective, and inexpensive. Your secretary will love you for them.

Finally, short paragraphs, short sentences, and short words make for short letters. They are also—as everybody from Hemingway to newspaper editors would agree—the most powerful form of the English language.

Step Three: Write for Results

Once you can bypass the trivia of letter writing, you can concentrate upon using your correspondence to get results. You think "communication" and not "correspondence" when you write executive-style letters.

> In your important letters, put your readers up front in your planning. What exactly do you want them to do or to think? Call on your knowledge of the psychology of motivation (Chapters 2–6) or direction giving (Chapter 7) to plan your message. Position your readers in your mind as if they were standing in front of you. Then get right into stating precisely what you want from them early and clearly in the letter. Make the pitch as personal as you can. Use his or her name in the text of the letter ("Therefore, Ellen, if you could ship the . . ."). Put the ball in the other person's court for action. An effective letter will leave the reader with the feeling of a need to act.

We're talking about your most important letters here, not the trivia letters (acknowledgments, confirmations, etc.), which you should have somebody else writing for you anyway. Write your important letters when you are thinking and feeling your best. They contain personal appeals. ("How shall *we* handle this problem, Ed. . . .") The reader knows without a question that they call for personal action.

If a letter is sufficiently important, consider these tactics for getting more attention:

- Append a handwritten note that reinforces your request.
- Mail it in an airmail envelope (only a device; mail goes by air anyway) or in an envelope marked "URGENT."
- Mail it under a priority delivery, e.g., special delivery, overnight guarantee, or via a commercial delivery service (the cost, although more than the first-class rate, may be trivial compared to what you want to accomplish).
- Use a home address if you feel it appropriate.
- Remember the power of a follow-up call.

HOW TO GET AHEAD IN WRITING DOCUMENTS AND REPORTS

None of us like that feeling of being stuck at the typewriter trying to write the first sentence of a critical report which, if it hits its mark, might open up whole new vistas for our career. We find ourselves rearranging our desks, getting more coffee, sharpening pencils, and doing everything except getting started. Usually we have no problem with knowing the main things we wish to get down. The difficulty is in getting started.

There is absolutely no reason for you to have a first-sentence hang-up. You can get around it by doing other things first. Try these four steps:

1. Plan with the *results* first.
2. *Organize* content from the top down.
3. Draft for *communication,* not composition.
4. Finish with the *professional* touch.

Step One:
Plan With the Results First

It is not unusual that we often find writing difficult. It is an artificial form of human communication. We must translate the highest of our ideas into inefficient sequences of marks on a page. This physical process is about ten times slower than the speed at which we can think up the language we want to use. And we often become so involved with the mechanics of word choice, spelling, and grammar that we forget about our main reason for doing all of this. That reason is not the document itself, but the results we want—what we want our readers to know or do after they read our document.

The next time you plan a document or report, take scratch paper and write out for yourself precisely what you want your readers to know or do as a result of reading what you write. (". . . so Jack at the Simpson Company will know the results of the market research on our new coffee. . . . why his sales could be terrific. . . . how Jack should handle the new brand right now. . . .") Next, plan backward from these results. What should be the form of the document and when must it be completed? Where will final production be done and what's the deadline (with a little leeway) for getting it there? What's my best writing schedule? (Set aside your prime intellectual time when you are at your best.)

If you can get your plans, including your production schedule, on 1 or 2 three-by-five-inch cards or a single sheet of paper, all the better. Try using a red felt-tip pen so you can see your plans when they are pinned on your wall. It's your game plan. Remember: *results!*

Step Two: Organize the Content From the Top Down

One key to fluent writing is to plan the content of your letter, not the exact text first. Plan ideas, not words. Don't worry about the first sentence.

Given the results you've jotted down in Step One, plan now what ideas or concepts will best help you to secure those results with your reader. Without worrying about the priority or sequence of these ideas, jot down a reminder note about each on a three-by-five-inch card. Next lay your cards out on a table in "top down" patterns according to the key ideas and the best supporting points. Jockey them around until they look the best to you. Use any arrangement that helps you visualize topic structures. (This does not have to be an outline.) Drop out anything that doesn't contribute to results (for the reader). Look for gaps in logical order; fill them in. (Yes, if you noticed it, this is the same way to plan a speech—Chapter 15.)

Get some help in brainstorming from a friend. Talk through the ideas with anybody who will listen and make suggestions. Try to do this as early as possible in the preparation process so your ideas can have a few days to incubate—it helps. Try the pushpin planning method used by designers and professional writers: Put your topic cards up on a large bulletin board or soft-faced wall. Use different-colored pins to identify related points. And right at the top of this, put your results and schedule cards. This is a terrific method for getting your content out in front so you can step back to see the full picture. It also makes you feel very productive. Don't worry about writing yet. Just *organize!*

Step Three:
Draft for Communication,
Not Composition

Your next task is to translate a table or wall full of cards into the sequential order of a document. If you think "communication" and "results," you'll surprise yourself with how naturally you can do this.

> Position your reader in your mind, as if he or she were sitting at a teletype machine and reading your words as they were typed out. Don't worry about introductions or conclusions at this point, just the body or key points of the report. Start writing on any main point that is the easiest for you. Don't get hung up on spelling or grammar. Use an approximate spelling for a difficult word, or use a synonym, or put in an underscored blank to fill in later. The point is to keep your main ideas flowing. Put the main points in the order you feel will be most effective for your reader. Get all you can of the body down on paper (or dictated). Keep your major blocks of draft writing on separate sheets of paper so you can easily rearrange them. Finally, draft an introduction and conclusion.

Try to do your drafting when you are rested and at your best. You will need your best creative juices. If it helps, get the translation process going by talking through the points in the order you think would be the clearest and most persuasive for your reader. Look at previous documents as possible models for organization.

Don't stop the flow of writing to quibble with mechanical details; fill them in later (just as a sculptor does). Remember the power of illustrations, charts, and tables. You can make the main point about a chart in your text, but leave the details for the illustration. Remember, too, that minor details can go in the appendix. Don't clutter up main points with trivia.

Think of the introduction as the place where you tell your reader what you are going to say in the main body of the report. In your conclusion, remind your reader of what you just said. If you get writer's block, try talking through the point (or another one). Or go get some rest. Remember: *Communicate!*

Step Four:
Finish With
the Professional Touch

It is usually best to edit on a day other than when you did the draft. Again, keep your reader foremost in mind. But also edit with the thought of who—secretary, printer—will be putting your document in finished shape.

If you are new to editing, take a few moments to look up the standard editing marks (many dictionaries have them, so do business or composition text-books); they will save you and your secretary time. Edit first for overall communication with your reader. Block out the major sections and sub-points. Next, move down to increasingly detailed levels to check word choices and sentence form. Do spelling last. You'll benefit, too, if you do not do all the editing at once. Plan final format when you edit; know what final draft form your secretary or printer will want for ease of handling. When you select a final format for typing or printing, including covers and possibly binding, have all blend in with your professional image.

You also need to be at your best when you edit. Do the overall content and stylistic editing when you are fresh. Save trivia like spelling for your less inspirational moods. Getting an associate to look over parts of your draft is sometimes helpful. Secretaries can also read the draft for general clarity. (Getting them involved before final typing also encourages them to give your document more of a personal commitment.) Again, standard proofing marks will keep communication clear between you and whoever must subsequently produce your document. (It is so much easier to give your secretary a standard guide to follow than for you to explain your editorial scrawls.) Printers like wide margins and absolutely everything double-spaced.

Consider prefacing your document with an "executive summary," preferably no longer than one page. Avoid dedication and acknowledgment pages ("Without the help of . . . etc."). They grow corny fast. Put everything important as early (up front) in the document as possible and the least important in the back, including in appendixes. Covers and bindings add to the professional look, but don't let them outdo the content of the report. Finally, know that the general appearance of your document is as important as the clothes you wear the day you present it. Look *professional*!

There are literally dozens of books and hundreds of schemes for planning your writing. If the above plan doesn't do the job for you, consult others. An hour or two of having a professional editor go over your style may be worth the cost. But for now, when you get ready to do your next report or document, think: *results, organize, communicate,* and *professional* (or "ROCpro" for short). It's a formula that works!

And when you finish that next report, ask yourself what writing the first sentence was like. You probably never even thought about it.

HOW TO BUILD YOUR EXECUTIVE WRITING STYLE

When you speak, only a limited number of individuals can hear you at one time. Also, the spoken word is elusive; it slips away in time. On the other hand, letters, documents, or reports are permanent records of your performance in management. As they accumulate, they generate a growing image of you as an executive. They portray your style.

What Is Your Written Image?

Do your important letters and reports stand out from those of others? How do people important to you perceive your style? Are you clear, readable, interesting, persuasive, positive, and personal?

An effective style doesn't come from inspiration or even so-called talent. It comes from know-how and plain hard work.

Ways to Build Your Style

Here are some tips to add to your know-how:

Get around hang-ups in grammar and spelling by tackling the problems directly. A few hours of review with a high school or college grammar book can pay real dividends (it will make more sense now). There are literally dozens of useful books on business writing. Many have helpful lists of common grammatical and spelling mistakes. A pocket-sized dictionary is invaluable for quick reference on meanings and spellings.

Strive for short paragraphs that emphasize a single point. (Sentences are individual complete statements that you make about a point.) Every paragraph should have an easily identifiable topic sentence which states the essence of the paragraph's point.

Use transition devices and other signposts to help your reader move from paragraph to paragraph. ("Therefore," "Moreover," "A further reason," etc.) Telling your reader directly about the organization of your message is often effective ("There are three reasons . . .").

Use short sentences. Avoid connecting simple sentences with and's or semicolons. Keep them simple. Sentences over twenty words in length are less readable than those in the optimum twelve-to-eighteen-word range.

Use short, meaningful words. Long words hinder readability. Avoid problems with technical terms when communicating across disciplines (e.g., an engineer writing to a person in marketing). Buy a pocket-sized copy of Roget's Thesaurus to aid you in selecting words. Avoid words so common that their meanings are bland (you can almost always improve upon "good").

Write in the present tense and use the active voice ("I sent the letters") rather than the passive ("The letters were sent by me"). Be as direct as possible.

Avoid filler language. "That" phrases ("during the time that," "until such time that," "despite the fact that") can almost always be reduced to one word (for the above, try "while," "until," and "although" respectively). "The fact that" can almost always be omitted.

Use the person's name and "you," "we," "I," and "us" pronouns if you want your letter to appeal personally to an individual ("I understand, Diane, how you feel about . . ."). If you want your reports to have more human interest, use words that refer to people, personal pronouns, and proper names. (Scenarios, examples involving people, and anecdotes are effective devices for improving the human-interest value of your writing.)

Assess the Readability
of Your Style

Test samples of your writing for their relative readibility by using the simple steps listed in the table at the end of this chapter. Interpret your own score relative to the guide given in the following table or, better yet, compare it with scores calculated on what you consider to be effective reports and letters in your organization.

READING-EASE SCORE	STYLE	TYPICAL MAGAZINE
90–10u	Very easy	Comics
80–90	Easy	Pulp fiction
70–80	Fairly easy	Slick fiction
60–70	Standard	Newsmagazines
50–60	Fairly difficult	*Harpers, Atlantic*
30–50	Difficult	Academic journals
0–30	Very difficult	Scientific reports

How to Use
the Readability Formula*

To estimate the readability ("reading ease") of a piece of writing, go through the following steps:

Step 1. Pick Your Samples
Unless you want to test a whole piece of writing, take samples. Take enough samples to make a fair test (say, three to five of an article and 25 to 30 of a book). Don't try to pick "good" or "typical" samples. Go by a strictly numerical scheme. For instance, take every third paragraph or every other page. (Ordinarily, the introductory paragraphs of a piece of writing are not typical of its style.) Each sample should start at the beginning of a paragraph.

Step 2. Count the Number of Words
Count the words in your piece of writing. If you are using samples, take each sample and count each word in it up to 100. Count contractions and hyphenated words as one word. Count numbers and letters as words, too, if separated by spaces. For example, count each of the following as one word: *1948, $19,892, e.g., C.O.D., wouldn't, week-end.*

*"How To Use the Readability Formula" (pp. 247–251) in *The Art of Readable Writing*, 25th Anniversary Edition, Revised and Enlarged by Rudolf Flesch. Copyright 1949, © 1974 by Rudolf Flesch. Reprinted by permission of Harper & Row, Publishers, Inc.

Step 3. Figure the Average Sentence Length

Figure the average sentence length in words for your piece of writing. If you are using samples, do this for all your samples *combined*. In a 100-word sample, find the sentence that ends nearest to the 100-word mark—that might be at the 94th word or the 109th word. Count the sentences up to that point and divide the number of words in those sentences in all your samples by the number of sentences in all your samples. In counting sentences, follow the units of thought rather than the punctuation: usually sentences are marked off by periods; but sometimes they are marked off by colons or semicolons—like these. (There are three sentences here between two periods.) But don't break up sentences that are merely joined by conjunctions like *and* or *but*.

Step 4. Count the Syllables

Count the syllables in your 100-word samples and divide the total number of syllables by the number of samples. If you are testing a whole piece of writing, divide the total number of syllables by the total number of words and multiply by 100. This will give you the number of syllables per 100 words. Count syllables the way you pronounce the word; e.g., *asked* has one syllable, *determined* three, and *pronunciation* five. Count the number of syllables in symbols and figures according to the way they are normally read aloud, e.g., two for *$* ("dollars") and four for *1916* ("nineteen sixteen"). However, if a passage contains several or lengthy figures, your estimate will be more accurate if you don't include these figures in your syllable count; in a 100-word sample, be sure to add instead a corresponding number of words after the 100-word mark. If in doubt about syllabication rules, use any good dictionary. (To save time, count all syllables except the first in all words of more than one syllable; then add the total to the number of words tested. It is also helpful to "read silently aloud" while counting.)

Step 5. Find Your "Reading Ease" Score

Using the average sentence length in words (*Step 3*) and the number of syllables per 100 words (*Step 4*), find your "reading ease" score on the READING EASE chart printed on page 144.

You can also use this formula:

Multiply the average sentence length by 1.015	. . . .
Multiply the number of syllables per 100 words by .846	. . . .
Add	
Subtract this sum from	206.835
Your "reading ease" score is	. . . .

The "reading ease" score will put your piece of writing on a scale between 0 (practically unreadable) and 100 (easy for any literate person).

20

Your Memory: How to Have One Like Flypaper

Did you know that one of the greatest arts of ancient times was memory training? But now in modern times our memory capabilities remain so under-developed that by the time we shake the second person's hand at a party we've forgotten the first one's name. You can improve your memory and it will be invaluable to you in the executive ranks. With a little training, you can become a whiz at remembering names. There are strategies for remembering what you want to say in a presentation or for remembering important things you have heard. You need not ever forget an important number again. Memory techniques do work. (Don't forget it!)

Patient: "Doctor, doctor, I have this dreadful problem. I can't remember things."
Doctor: "How long have you had this problem?"
Patient: "What problem?"

SWEET MEMORIES OF SUCCESS

In her short five years on the sales team of a leading office-equipment dealer, Sandy W. was making a name for herself. Her annual sales reached the seven-figure mark in her fifth year with the company. But more than this, she was becoming a kind of legend around the business for her performance in sales presentations. One reason was that she was able to quote a great variety of equipment specs from memory. Another was that she always made a habit of remembering names when meeting clients the first time around at a sales meeting—sometimes up to fifty of them.

In a seminar while she was working on her MBA, Sandy wrote a paper on what she had attempted to do to build a winning sales technique. Among the strategies was to use her memory more effectively. First, she made a serious attempt to remember the key features of all new equipment which she was representing. Second, she tried to anticipate what important questions might be asked by customers, then she made sure she had the answers well in mind. Finally, she consciously tried to remember the names of her clients at their very first meeting.

Does Sandy have some kind of photographic memory? Superior brain capacity? Not at all. She simply uses a few simple memory strategies which you can learn from this chapter and put into use immediately. These strategies are based upon fundamental principles about human memory. Best of all, you can easily learn them. Once you know a few, it is important to practice them and even more important to have the ambition to use them in practical situations where memory can improve your communication power. We will describe strategies that will improve your ability to remember names, lists, dates, and numbers, as well as what you hear in a talk or what you want to say.

HOW TO REMEMBER NAMES IMPORTANT TO YOU

People like being called by name. When you remember a customer's, client's, or new associate's name right off, they will usually feel that you are taking a special interest in them. Remembering names is not very difficult if you make a conscious effort. Here are some strategies.

Visualize What a Name "Names"

Several memory principles make recalling names easier than you might think. A combination of two principles works well for names. First, try to associate the name with a mental image rather than its word form. Second, the more bizarre or silly you can make this association, the better are the chances that you will remember the name.

> Try to make an immediate visualization upon hearing a name that directly suggests an image. If you can remember the image, then chances are good that you will remember the name. The sillier the image, the better.

Sometimes this works for a combination of the first and last names. What kinds of images do names like Frank Stone, Henry Fisch, or Gloria Armstrong conjure up for you? Frank Stone could suggest an image of a stone with a design carved in it for putting the cancellation on letters. (I warned you that these would be bizarre!) You can even add to that image the figure of Frank Stone banging down the "stone" on a letter. We probably have the same immediate image for Mr. Fisch. You can add the Henry by thinking of him dressed in an Oh Henry! candy-bar wrapper. And, of course, create a face on the fish that looks remarkably like Henry himself. There are a lot of

Armstrongs; the name might remind you of the Arm and Hammer logo on the baking soda box. Now frame this logo in one of those religious picture frames from a medieval cathedral and there's no way you'll forget Gloria (especially if you have Gloria's face looking down from the upper part of the frame).

Practice Creating Unique Visualizations

Some names are not so immediately helpful. Walter Komsky, Susan Johnston, or Robert Wilson are names which require us to be more imaginative. We can still try to conjure up a quick image as with the earlier names, but this takes a little practice.

> In your spare moments practice fitting imaginative visualizations with names that are not the same or similar to common words. Practicing this will increase your ability to create an on-the-spot visualization when you want to remember a name in a hurry.

You could remember Walter at first as somebody who wanted you to "come and ski." Of course, he has on ski clothes. Susan is from "John's town." The name *Wilson* can suggest a person (the image of good old Robert) writing out a will for his son. If you have a roster of names of important individuals whom you'll be meeting at an important gathering, you can practice some visual associations ahead of time.

Create an Image From Face or Body Features

A person's face, dress, or body image can suggest a visualization, especially if there is something unique about a feature.

> When you meet somebody new, study that person's face and body for a moment in order to detect any outstanding or unusual characteristic. Try to associate the name and this characteristic with some type of silly image, maybe even a kind of cartoon.

Somebody with a rather prominent nose may have a sound like *be* (beak), *sm* (smell), *pro* (proboscis), *sn* (snout, snoot, sniff), or *no* in their name. You might make up names like the famous writer Damon Runyon used for his bookies and other hustlers—Big Sam the Crapshooter, Larry the Lip, Seldom-seen Sarah, Harried Hilda, or Mary the Canary. Immediately visualize the caricature and you'll have a good chance of remembering the name. You'll have to practice this technique, but it's fun and it works. (Don't slip and call your boss Randy Rat Lips in a loose moment!)

Be Certain to Hear
the Name Correctly

All the memory techniques in the world won't help you if you did not understand a name accurately in the first place. In fact, it may often be better not to remember a name than to call Margarita "Sally." You'll be insulting one of her most precious possessions—her name.

> Listen especially closely to names. Don't hesitate to ask for a name to be repeated, especially by the person himself. If you still don't get it, ask for a spelling.

It's fair game the first time around to ask for a name to be repeated. This may be especially important if a third party has done the introduction and may have slurred the pronunciation. A brief conversation about a name will help you to remember it. Also, don't hesitate to ask a person for his or her business card. Finally, if you have to ask for a spelling, hope that the name isn't Smith or Jones!

You are probably already aware that you can carry these memory techniques to great lengths so as to remember literally hundreds of names. Some people even make a living at it as entertainers. But this requires much practice and probably more effort than it is worth for you. For now, why not set a minimum goal of not forgetting as many names as you usually do. A few minutes' practice now and then with the above strategies will easily do the job for you.

HOW TO REMEMBER
ITEMS AND LISTS

Visualizations, especially bizarre ones, are also a very helpful memory principle for remembering lists of items. Images of some overall relational or organizational layout can also be an aid for remembering individual items. For now, we'll describe how you can use these principles for re-membering lists of items.

Develop Image Composites

Visualizing items in some unusual combined image is an easy method for remembering items that may not be logically related to one another. Image composites are especially helpful in on-the-spot conversations where you can't take notes or where you haven't prepared some memory device ahead of time.

> Combine individual items into a composite visualization—the more humor-
> ous, unusual, or bizarre, the better. Practice generating these combinations in
> spare moments when you are waiting in line, riding the subway, or stopped at
> a traffic light. You'll then have the strategy ready to go when you need it.

Suppose you meet your boss in the hallway and he says that he wants the
company annual report; the latest newsletter; and separate brochures on
your lines of film developing chemicals, photo frames, felt-tip pens, super
glues, and photocopy paper sent out to the Franklin Company immediately. The strategy is to generate an image that will hold this list together in
your memory, a strategy that combines the items. Again, the sillier it is, the
easier it will be to remember.

One simple composite would be to visualize a kind of Ben Franklin
character (big head, long hair, cartoon body, the usual "busy" figure with
stuff hanging all over him). You could have him carrying all the items on
your list—pens over his ears, annual report under one arm, the newsletter
in the other, a handful of copy paper with bottles of photochemicals and
super glues balanced on top, and a picture frame around his neck.

Try the "Location" Method

Another way to relate a group of items is to visualize them placed around in
a room or space very familiar to you—thus, the name "location."

> Visualize individual items as if they were placed in some illogical or silly place
> in your living room, bedroom, office, or anyplace that is familiar to you in
> great detail. The sillier the better.

Take, for example, the Franklin Company order we just mentioned. You
might visualize the items placed around your bedroom. Don't imagine the
photochemicals sitting on your bedside table, but instead on your pillow
(extra unusual). Have the felt-tip pens sticking out of your reading lamp, the
photocopy paper hanging from the ceiling, the brochures tucked in for the
night in your bed, and so on. This, also, is a quickie technique that is fun to
practice in off moments. Try it next time you make up a list for the grocery
store. Be sure to have the food items visualized all over your living room,
not the kitchen. That would be too logical!

Create Visual Image Links
or Chains

This method uses images to associate items in pairs, then pairs with one
another, so you have a chain of associated items. It is handy for remembering a sequence of items.

Visualize some bizarre combination of the first two items on the 'list. Then combine the second item in an image with a third, the third with a fourth, and so on. If you have the opportunity, run the chain of images through your mind a few times—backward as well as forward.

Suppose that during a formal luncheon in a Middle Eastern country, a high-level official mentions five aspirations he has for his nation. You want to remember these in their order of priority so you can cite them in subsequent business correspondence. Yet you do not want to be so obvious at the moment as to write them down. The aspirations include upgrading health care, providing free education through primary school, doubling agricultural output, constructing an artificial seaport, and keeping politically neutral in international affairs.

You might first visualize a cartoonlike image of a child from that country being examined by a doctor while through a window you can also see a new schoolhouse. (The prominence of the medical scene is a cue that it has priority over the school one.) The next image could be a school with big piles of grain in the background. Another could be big piles of grain being loaded onto a ship in an apparently new port. And the final image could be that same port with ships of politically different countries in it. Try visualizing this example or one of your own. You'll be surprised at how easily they work, especially for remembering the order. Note that once you have the chain in mind, it's about as easy listing it backward as forward.

Make the Meaningless Meaningful

Words or phrases that have no immediate meaning to us are especially difficult to remember. Sometimes this occurs when a technical term is used by the other person or a word in a foreign language is slipped into the context. Such words can trip up your attempts to remember lists. The best strategy for this problem is to try to remember the sound pattern of the word; keep this in mind until you can get some help with a definition or translation.

> To remember a word that has no immediate meaning to you, think of a word or words in your own language that have a similar sound (phonetic) pattern. This strategy makes the abstract word concrete for you. Then visualize an image for this word that you do know.

Our phonetic memories are very powerful if a sound pattern is associated with a meaning. (Remember how you can sometimes remember the sound of the beginning of a name or word, but cannot remember the rest of it?) As a consequence, anytime you can associate sounds with a meaning, you will have a powerful memory strategy. Suppose that a speaker used the term *heterophily* in a seminar on marketing research. Maybe something as bizarre as "hit a trough in Philly" (Philadelphia) would help you to remember the sound approximation of the word.

You have probably already used variations of this technique for learning new words of a foreign language and associating them with meanings in your own language. For example, a word sounding like *sahd* in Russian means "garden." That this sounds like *sod* in English can help you make the meaning association.

Use Prompt-Word Codes

You have probably already used a prompt-word scheme in studying for exams in school. It is a helpful strategy when you have time to work out the word.

> Form a memory "prompt word" by combining the first letters of words that describe the items on a list you wish to remember. If the prompt word itself is meaningful (and even silly), you'll remember it more easily.

If you read Chapter 19 on writing, do you remember "ROCPro," meaning *results, organization, communication,* and *professional?* It was a prompt-word scheme.

HOW TO REMEMBER IMPORTANT NUMBERS AND DATES

Numbers are naturally difficult to remember because until they are associated with something, they are abstractions. Memory principles used for recalling numbers mostly involve strategies for making numbers meaningful. Most of these methods are a bit more complicated than the memory strategies we have described. They will require a little practice. For most of us, it is best to write down important numbers. This is more reliable and requires less effort than number memory schemes. However, here are some simple schemes so at least you can remember what to write down. They will also be useful when you want to remember numbers for use in speeches and stand-up presentations.

Learn a Word-Peg System for Numbers

Words are easier to remember than numbers, so some memory schemes for numbers involve converting them into meaningful words, which then serve as memory pegs. One strategy is to develop words that contain sounds you associate with numerical digits.

Develop or adopt a scheme whereby each of the digits 1 through 9 (and 0) is associated with a consonant sound. Memorize this scheme. Then when you want to remember a number, create a meaningful (peg) word from the associated consonants plus any vowels you need.

Memory expert Harry Lorayne suggests the following scheme*:

NUMBER	SOUND	TIP FOR REMEMBERING—
1.	t, d	t has 1 vertical line
2.	n	typewritten n has 2 lines
3.	m	typewritten m has 3 lines
4.	r	four ends in r
5.	L	Roman numeral L = 50
6.	j, ch, sh, soft g,	written J, is backward 6
7.	k, hard c, hard g	upside-down 7 written over a regular one looks a little like K
8.	f, v	lowercase written f has two loops like 8
9.	p, b	backwards p looks like a 9
0.	s, z	sounds like zero

You can remember the above associations almost instantly by remembering the simple phrase, "TeN MoRe LoGiC FiBs."

Now suppose that you wanted to remember the stock number of a new piece of equipment—147140. Using the above sound associations, you'd have T R C T R S, which could give you *TRACTORS,* and an easily remembered image. If the piece of equipment was a paint nozzle, you might visualize a composite of tractors being painted. Or the tractor image could be used in a memory chain of some type. You can remember many numbers and complex ones by this system, but it will take a little practice to do it quickly. (Look away from the page a moment and see if simply by remembering the phrase about "fibs," you can now remember the system.)

Convert Long Numbers Into Visual Composites

Although there are many good reasons to write down long numbers, sometimes we just do not have the chance. The telephone operator may spew out an important number for us while we're in a phone booth without paper or pencil. Together with the area code, that's ten numbers to

How to Develop a Super-Power Memory (New York: New American Library, 1974), adapted by permission of Frederick Fell Publishers, Inc.

remember. We'll hear important ZIP codes and street addresses too fast to write them down. Or, like Sandy Wilson, we'll want to remember a few product codes or prices without having to shuffle through papers while making a presentation.

> Use a word peg system to convert phone numbers, ZIP codes, street numbers, or product codes for prices into composite visualizations. Include in the composite important associations you wish to make with the number.

Suppose at a cocktail party you hear that a customer's new address is 721 9th Street. You want to make a mental note of it without disrupting the ongoing conversation. With the consonant sound system, you might immediately think "K N T—B." One visualization would be a knot in the shape of a *B*. You could "tie in" with this your client's face, his company's logo, or anything that would stick in your memory. If you practice this method in spare moments, you'll surprise yourself by how fast you can use it. In the years to come, with more complex zip codes, as we pay bills by pushing numbers on our telephones, and as we work more directly with electronic computers, these schemes will be all the more useful to you. But remember that many numbers are still worth writing down. (One of my friends tangled with the IRS for eighteen months because he had used three variations of his Social Security number in reporting income from consulting!)

Use Digit Word Pegs for Dates

Remembering important appointments, due dates, or even birthdays can be made easy by word-peg images.

> Convert dates into digits, then use word pegs to generate visual composites which also include the reason for remembering the date.

You can remember days of the week by associating them with their numerical order. Begin with either Sunday or Monday, whichever you think of as the first day. If you want to remember to catch a flight on Sunday the twenty-fifth (1—25), you could use the consonant sound system to develop a key word like *Toe—Nail* (remember that the vowels don't mean anything). If you needed to remember that this was in June, you might add *Joe* (*J* for sixth month), then think of all this in some silly composite of a "Joe Toenail" at the airport for your flight. (0 can stand for the tenth month, October, but you'll have to decide upon some method for November and December. This could be *TT*, a special double sound for November, and *TN*, embellished with jingle bells, for December.)

HOW TO REMEMBER
WHAT YOU READ OR HEAR

All methods for improved reading or listening comprehension (perhaps you've already read Chapter 17 or 18) include methods for helping you to organize what you perceive. These same methods carry over to memory strategies.

Image Chains or Composites Will Help

When you do not have time to take notes or to work up a more complicated or detailed memory scheme, rapid visualizations will help you to remember what you read or hear, especially sequences of ideas, items, or events.

> Extract the main ideas of what you hear and create an image association for each. Link the images through the chain, location, or general composite method.

Of course, it's not always easy to pick out the main ideas. The material may be unclear, disorganized, or dull in the first place. But once you begin pulling out the main ideas, you'll want to get them into a memory scheme fast. Suppose that upon hearing or reading a consultant's report on public reaction to a new brand of freeze-dried coffee, you sense that the main points are: "tastes good," "doesn't look dark enough when brewed," "too expensive," "brand logo looks attractive," and "customer would like to keep the container for other use." You could visualize a cartoon face smiling as coffee is sipped, but the eyes are looking down and frowning at the sight of it. In the next link, the frowning eyes could be associated with an empty wallet, and so on. On the other hand, perhaps you could combine all the main ideas in one composite image. The chain method could also be used to keep the ideas in some order—priority of importance, for example.

Using any of these methods will pay several dividends. For one, simply the intent to remember main ideas by some method will keep your attention more sharpened for detecting them in the spoken or written material. Also, the chances are usually good that if you can recall the main ideas, these in turn will serve to jog your memory for more details if you want them. But simply remembering main ideas does not always aid you in remembering relations among them, except for their sequential order. Often, the essence of complex materials is in the relations among the ideas, not just in the ideas themselves.

Use Visual Organization Patterns to Remember Relations

Because the organization among complex ideas is an abstraction, we can usually remember it better if we try to remember it in terms of a concrete visual image.

> Develop some standard visual organization formats for your memory strategy repertoire. Employ them for organizing what you wish to remember about the relationships among ideas in what you read or hear.

Sometimes visual organization schemes can suggest a very standard format—cause and effect, for example:

_____

_____   _____

_____   PLUS   _____   EQUALS   _____

_____   _____

_____

_____

You might find it useful to visualize ideas as they represent a hierarchy, as in a standard outline format:

I. _____

   A. _____

      1. _____

      2. _____

   B. _____

II. _____

   A. _____

   B. _____

   C. _____

Sometimes you can work up composites of visual images and outline forms, including the location strategy. You might recall the ideas in a financial report by locating them in different positions on a dollar bill, the position of several new members of a company by visualizing their faces on the organization chart, or an item of information from a printed page by its location in the page format. Again, the principle is that visual memory works well for us. It is the best memory strategy for remembering complex relations among ideas.

If the number memory schemes work well for you, they can also be used to help in the organization of ideas that you hear in a larger spoken or written context. If you use the consonant-sounds method, then the first idea you wish to remember should be associated with a word starting or ending with *t* (remember? the sound for 1).

HOW TO REMEMBER
WHAT YOU WANT TO SAY

As we warned in Chapter 15, try to avoid the word-for-word memorization of speeches. But you can try to remember the sequence of ideas.

Reduce Your Main Ideas
to Key Words

What are the key thoughts, points, actions, or attitudes that you want your listener not only to hear, but to take away from your presentation?

> Select a key word with especially high visual potential for each main idea of your presentation. Write these key words down in the sequence of your speech. Develop interesting visualizations for them. Keep the visualization in the back of your mind as you think through that part of your speech or practice delivering it.

In a presentation to a group of university alumni on the topic of communication effectiveness, I used these key words:

Football: Opening joke about disastrous season

TV: Attention-getting statistics on how many hours a day our children watch television

Student: Theme-setting story of young graduate who kept botching up job interviews

Three V's: What interviewer said about looks, voice, and language of young man

Visual: How we look sometimes says more than our words

Vocal: Even how we sound often says as much as what words we use

Verbal: What's left for words

Emily: Wrap-up inspirational example of success against all odds.

It is not difficult to conjure up images for these words; they all have high visual potential. The faces of the student and Emily are easily visualized, as is the football. Since I often talk about the three V's, I really do not have to create images for them (as you will not have to do for ideas very familiar to you). With these key words and images I have a powerful tool for remembering what I want to say.

Now what we need is to put these images into a memory scheme.

Use a Memory Scheme for Your Key Words

> Put the images of your key words into a memory chain, a composite image or a location scheme as a prompting device for remembering the main ideas you plan to express.

If you use the composite image or location methods, then be sure that they will also provide you with cues as to the sequence of your ideas. You'll find one extra advantage in the memory chain. It's so easy to remember it backward and forward that if you digress from your main ideas or stop to answer questions, you'll have little trouble examining your sequence of ideas in order to pick up the train of thought again.

> Consider using a key-word spelling scheme to remember your main ideas. Form an overall memory prompt word from the first letters of each of your key words.

If I used a prompt word for the above example, it would probably be something like "FS 3V E."

> Try combining the key words for your talk in order in the form of a sentence, even a nonsense one. (For example, "Football on TV wrecked the student's visual, vocal, and verbal skills, said Emily.")

One final use of the key-word memory scheme is to suggest it to your listeners so they can remember even better what you have tried to tell them. (Now put the book aside and see if you can remember the main points of my speech.)

YOU CAN PUT YOUR MEMORY TO WORK

Most of us do not have poor memories, we simply fail to use our capacity effectively. The strategies given in this chapter require almost no study, and all can be practiced in your spare moments or tried on tasks like grocery lists before you try them in a board meeting. Moreover, effective memory techniques will give you added confidence in your work and in your everyday relations with others.

And don't forget the power of remembering names. Although Sandy W. is not the real name of the young woman who inspired the success story for this chapter, I have felt free to use her nickname, which is impossible to forget. Some of the people around the office used to kid Sandy by calling her "the gal with the flypaper memory"!

V

MAKE YOUR NEW
POWER PAY

Communication power goes beyond writing more effective letters, getting up in front of people, or in having improved basic skills. Why not focus that power on your long-range goals? Then use your new communication power to move toward them. Getting there is half the fun.

21

Plan For Success

If you are more successful today with your communication power, is it building toward success for tomorrow? Without long-range goals, your little successes will seldom count toward big ones. Are you in a hurry going nowhere? The goal-setting exercise in this chapter can improve your aim toward long-range success. What you plan for tomorrow will affect what you do today. That is your ultimate investment of executive communication power.

HOW TO SET PERSONAL GOALS

Sure, you have always had ideas of where you wanted to go in life, but have you ever taken the time to write down your goals? Have you thought of the difference between life goals, the intermediate goals you'll need to fulfill in order to reach the life goals, and what you'll do tomorrow morning in order to get started on your new plan?

Try this exercise: Go someplace comfortable where you will not be disturbed. Or take a one-day sabbatical to someplace you enjoy. Then do the following:

Take three sheets of paper and label each as follows:
  1. Life Goals
  2. Intermediate Goals
  3. Tomorrow's Plan
Refer to the following three sections as you fill in these sheets.

1. Life Goals

You are seventy and have been most successful. A leading movie producer wants to make a film of your life. What will you want to have been known for?

Think about:
- personal satisfaction and happiness
- making others happy
- the respect of others
- the contribution of something valuable to humanity
- wealth
- your career as an example for others
- spiritual fulfillment
- achievement in your profession
- the job you've done with your children
- your place in history
- creativity

Outline or sketch out your life goals on sheet number one. Restrict yourself to the front of that sheet only. It will make you set priorities.

2. Intermediate Goals

The film producer says "fine" to your description of your long-range success. But he presses you for your story. What did you do to get where you got?

Use sheet number two for your notes. Consider:
- self-evaluations to set new courses of action
- your ability to set your sights high
- getting big decisions (even dramatic ones) made and implemented
- taking risks
- people who may be influential to your success
- your ability to understand organizations you work for
- balance in your life between materialistic and spiritual (or philosophic) ends
- special skills acquired
- a willingness to accept, even to take advantage of, change
- confidence in yourself
- a supportive family life, circle of friends, or both
- extra-hard work, dedication
- how you feel about your ethics; your comfort with them
- standing up for your rights or the rights of others
- your ability to take losses and to learn from them

Write or list a scenario of what you need to do to reach the success you want—

or the ingredients of an exciting yet believable script for the producer. Again, stick to one page.

3. Plans for Tomorrow

The producer wants to begin your life story with the age you actually are right now. Moreover, he wants the opening scene to be tomorrow morning.

So from your hypothetical vantage point of seventy years of age, and basking in success, think back to your current age and project yourself into tomorrow morning. How do your life goals and intermediate goals influence what you plan to do tomorrow? Will your producer friend have a dramatic opening scene?

Think about how your plans for tomorrow fit your goals. Use sheet number three for notes.

- What will you do tomorrow that will help you toward your intermediate or long-range goals?
- What will you start cutting out of your life tomorrow because it is getting you nowhere?
- Will your day be rescheduled after you think of your goals?

Consider, too, how what you may be doing tomorrow contributes to your personal growth and fitness, a goal we humans share as a fundamental psychological motive.

- What will you be doing that will improve your mind?
- How can you improve your physical fitness?
- What will make you happy?
- What will improve your relations with others and make them happy ("you win—I win" situations)?
- Will you take a few moments to review the day, to see how well things have gone—to enjoy what has gone right and to take steps to change what has gone wrong?

And for your personal communication, answer these questions:

- Will your communications be focused on personal and professional goals?
- Which people you are dealing with tomorrow are important in your goals (including family and friends)?
- Can you use new powers for personal motivation so that these people can help you achieve your goals as well as their own?
- Will you apply any new strategies for winning in typical communication situations?
- Will you use more effectively your powers of speech, body language, listening, reading, writing, or memory?

Feel free to use more than just one side of sheet number three for tomorrow's plans because . . .

It might be a terrific opening scene!

Index